I0469145

Money
Well Saved

Money
Well Saved

Seven Steps
Towards Greater
Financial Peace of Mind

Wallace R. Curiel

...for Mom and Dad...

All questions of a legal, accounting or financial nature should be
addressed to an appropriate professional in the field. This book is
intended solely for the entertainment of the reader.

MONEY WELL SAVED
Published by Transcendental Media Group Press.
ISBN: 978-0-6151-6661-2

Copyright © 2025 by Wallace R. Curiel.
All rights reserved.
No part of this book may be used or reproduced in any manner
whatsoever without written permission except in the case
of brief quotations embodied in articles for review.

Printed in the United States of America.

10 9 8 7 6 5 4 3 2 1

Preface

*One must not always think about what one must
do but, rather, what one should be.*

—Meister Eckhart

Once upon a time, at the not *too* ripe old age of thirty-five, I found myself unemployed, over fifty thousand dollars in debt, and living in the basement bedroom of my brother's house in Alexandria, VA. I had just moved there from my hometown of San Diego, CA.

I had decided to make the move to improve my chances of re-starting my career working for the US Federal Government, a career I had abandoned over two years earlier to start a business. Alexandria is in the Washington, DC metro area and there were and are a lot Federal jobs there.

So, anyway, there I was, thousands of miles from home, broke, unemployed, in debt *and* imposing on the kindness of family but, unfortunately, that was not to be the low point of my financial life. The low point came a few days after I actually got hired back into the Federal Government not a month after arriving in Virginia.

By this time I was pretty much living off of a couple of credit cards that were not (*I thought*) maxed out and yet, to thank a fellow employee at my new place of employment for showing me around the place, introducing me to others and helping me get settled in, I offered to buy her lunch.

The meal, itself, went just fine and, when the check came, I glanced at the total and handed the waiter a credit card. In a matter of minutes, however, the waiter returned (and with the manager, no less) and announced to us and to everyone within earshot that the card had been declined. The manager then *requested* that we pay in cash in order to "avoid further confusion," as he put it.

Digging through our pockets, counting out bills and loose change on the table, my lunch guest and I were able to come up with just enough cash between us to cover the tab. Meanwhile, the manager and our waiter stood there, hovering over us like we were a couple of deadbeats when, really, it was more like one deadbeat and one innocent bystander.

Slinking out of that restaurant, feeling like every eye in the place was on us, it was that moment right there that *was* the low point in my financial life. When I look back on that moment now, I realize that, as low points go, that incident was not like going bankrupt or losing your home to foreclosure, but it was, nevertheless, a rather rude awakening. And, to this day, I still cringe when I think about it.

I do not know if everything happens for a reason but what happened in that restaurant that afternoon is what provided me the motivation I needed to finally get my financial house in order. And the fact that I have lived through difficult financial times has given me a real empathy with those now living through their own.

Can someone who has never had that sort of moment, or reached the financial depths I was at, ever really understand the pain that poor money management can cause a person? I'm not sure...education and degrees and initials after your name...well, absolutely, they do count for something but, really, they only go so far.

And, no, you don't need a weatherman to know which way the wind blows, but it helps, I think, to have faced a storm or two. In fact, I almost think that the only people who should counsel others about managing money are those who have been there and done that.

Anyway, night had fallen by the time I left work. When I got back to my brother's place, I retreated to the basement and sat there on the edge of the bed with no lights on, alone and in the dark, trying to figure out how I had come to this.

The thought came to me that, by that time in my life, I had been working for over fifteen years—a long time, I realized!—and it made me wonder just how much I had earned, in total, during all those years.

Doing the math in my head, the number came to something like five-hundred thousand dollars! To this day I can clearly remember the feeling that hit me when I arrived at that figure—I was, literally, dumbstruck. And, then, I got mad! How could I have made so much money and, yet, have absolutely nothing to show for it? And, actually, if you considered my debts, I had less than nothing!

As I sat there thinking, I remembered something I had heard or read somewhere about how you should always save at least ten percent of your income. As I considered that thought, it came to me how different my situation would be if I had only managed to do that.

For one thing, instead of being broke, I would have had over fifty thousand dollars in the bank and I'm sure you can see how that would have changed everything. But the sad truth is that, up to that point in my life, I had never really given much thought to saving money.

Later, when I thought about it some more, I could not remember anyone ever explaining the importance of saving money to me—either at home or at any school I had ever attended. And it's not that I'm blaming anyone other than myself but a little help along these lines, somewhere along the line, might well have helped me avoid what came to pass.

So, not knowing any better, I had simply earned money and spent it with absolutely no consideration for the future. If I had some left over at the end of the month, it only meant that I could splurge a little. When I think about how I managed my finances back then, it is not only embarrassing, it is almost painfully so.

In that moment, I had a revelation of sorts. And, although I could not have defined it real well back then, I know now that it was simply this—you need a plan for every dollar you earn. That night was also the start of what became a long journey of learning to manage my personal finances more wisely. And the first step in that journey was a commitment to building my savings account.

The day I finally (*finally!*) got my first paycheck at my new job, the first thing I did was to make a deposit to my savings account. And I have been a committed saver ever since. And it was about that same time that I began to read every book I could find on personal financial management because, although that little fiasco in the restaurant provided me with the motivation I needed to want to change, I knew that I would need to learn the skills necessary to do so.

I did, eventually, learn what I needed to learn about money but it was not quick and it was certainly not easy...I had a lot to learn. And the foundation of that strategy was, and still is, to simply manage my income to grow my savings steadily over time.

There are any number of good reasons to save some part of every dollar you earn but, perhaps, the best is that nothing will enhance your financial peace of mind quite like money in the bank.

In this book, I will share with you what I wish I had known about managing my money way back when...when what I did not know had left me, both literally and figuratively, in the dark. And I can only hope that the lessons of *Money Well Saved* reach you before you reach the point I was at...once upon a time.

.

Money Well Saved

TABLE OF CONTENTS

Introduction

*Financial security and peace of mind are
inseparably linked and, until you feel secure
about your finances, that faint dread of living
too close to the edge will always be there.*

—Wallace R. Curiel

Let me tell you how I came to write this book. I once taught personal financial management at the college level. Now, back in the days when I was living in my brother's basement, that did not seem like the place I was headed but there I was, not too many years later, doing just that.

The classes were held in the evening and the students were almost all working adults and older than the typical college student. As we progressed through the semester, it became obvious to me that the curriculum for the course was not addressing the real needs of the students. And, believe me, I knew their real needs because not too long ago I had been searching for the answers to the same financial issues they were now facing.

The course was very broad in scope and briefly touched on almost every imaginable facet of the subject. And, although I know it was not what was intended, the result was that no single topic received the attention it deserved.

In particular, the time we spent on the fundamentals of personal financial management was insufficient to cover the subject adequately. But the fundamentals are what provide the foundation for a lifetime of sound money management and, in discussions with my students, I soon came to realize that the issues that concerned them the most all had to do with the fundamentals—you know, topics such as how to budget and how to save, how to reduce debt and how to measure your progress when it comes to managing your money.

Many of my students also expressed the concern that money was the source of a lot of stress in their lives and, that although they thought about money all the time, it seemed like they simply could not figure out how to manage their money to achieve those goals that mattered to them most.

Most of them managed to pay the bills and keep food on the table but they were all convinced that there had to be more to life, and money, than that. And they were right—financial peace of mind is not achieved simply by being able to make ends meet. That is an important first step, of course, but it is not nearly enough.

What it takes to feel at peace about your finances is a sense that you are in control of your money and to know that both today and tomorrow are being accounted for. I wrote this book, then, to meet not only the needs of people like my students but of anyone who feels they should be or could be doing better, financially.

I also wrote this book for anyone whose finances are keeping them awake at night. You see, I know that peace of mind is getting harder and harder to come by and that life seems to keep getting more and more complicated and faster paced. So, whatever you can do to reduce *any* anxiety in your life will just naturally have the effect of increasing your peace of mind, in general.

The list of all the possible individual causes of stress in our lives is long but, for many of us, money problems are at the top of that list. Most of us just sort of assume that more money would be the answer to all our financial worries but, as simple as it seems, more money can actually make matters worse!

You see, if more money *was* the answer then all our money problems would disappear as our income increased over time. But they don't, do they? So how does it happen that we take our money problems with us even as we earn more? It is because, in the *real* world, our spending is almost always growing right along with our income.

In fact, many times our spending will grow faster than our income and our level of financial peace of mind will actually diminish as we earn more! So, even though we are making more money, the difference is often not enough to keep up with the increases in our spending.

Debt is a big factor in how much stress we experience due to our personal finances and nothing puts you at risk of incurring debt like living right up to the limits of your income. And, when you live like that, you will never be able to save and accumulate a ready cash reserve sufficient to get you through a lengthy financial downturn.

A lack of savings is a sure sign that you are living way too close to the financial edge and it is obviously not a situation conducive to your peace of mind. One cause of financial stress that has reached epidemic proportions in our society is the growing anxiety many of us are experiencing because we know that we are not saving enough to *ever* retire.

Even if we had the option of working to our last breath, I doubt many of us will actually want to do so. That being the case, you must save for that time in your life when you will need a source of income to replace the income you now earn by working for a living.

And retirement is only the *primary* long-term goal of financial planning. A sound financial plan will include several other long-term *and* short-term financial goals, as well.

Certainly, we can all acknowledge that just keeping the lights on and the bills paid is a blessing but there is more to a full life than that—our dreams must also be considered in our financial planning if they are ever to be realized.

Whether it's a summer wandering around Europe, a cabin in the mountains, or, simply, one day being able to kiss the rat race goodbye, our dreams almost all come with a price tag attached. But a dream will stay just that, just a dream, unless you have a plan for turning it into reality.

A certain amount of your financial peace of mind does depend on how secure you feel about your present financial situation, but the future also plays a role in that equation.

If you are managing to meet today's expenses but you are not saving enough to secure your financial future, then a sense of dread in your life is all but inevitable. And, if your dreams are going unaccounted for, then it is also likely that you will find yourself living with a sense of hopelessness, as well.

It is often the case that the source of much of our financial discontent is not actually our income but, rather, our spending. Many of us spend so much of what we earn that it does not allow for any savings at all, much less enough to both secure the future and finance our dreams. And many of us are actually going into debt so that we can spend even *more* than we earn!

Nothing can increase your level of financial anxiety like using credit cards to prop up your income because you live knowing that the day of reckoning is bound to arrive. And, yet, that's exactly what more and more of us are doing.

This damage to our financial well-being is, however, largely self-inflicted. I mean, after all, it is not as if someone is forcing us to live beyond our means. We do it to ourselves and, as we dig our hole deeper and deeper, we surrender yet another measure of financial peace of mind with every shovel full.

But regardless of how much stress your personal finances are causing you today, there *are* steps you can take to begin to relieve your anxiety. And not one of those steps will require that you earn more money. You don't need to get a second job or work weekends to achieve greater financial peace of mind because more money is not the answer. The answer is more savings.

Too many of us get way too caught up in the getting and spending of today to the extent that we completely lose sight of tomorrow. But if you do that, eventually, you will arrive at a moment that will be like waking up from any other sort of over-indulgent binge. And, almost always, there will be a hefty price to pay. A price, I might add, you can't afford.

The opposite of financial peace of mind is financial anxiety. Feeling anxious about money is all too common these days. Anxiety is a form of stress but stress is not an entirely bad thing. In fact, stress is a biological self-defense mechanism. We experience stress when we are at risk. Stress can be a signal telling you that a change is in order.

So, the fact is, a *little* stress is a good thing and totally natural. It keeps us alert and vigilant and that is how we should be when it comes to preserving our financial well-being—alert and vigilant. The fact is that there will never be a time in your life when money will not require your diligent attention.

On the other hand, money shouldn't be any harder than it has to be and there are steps you can take to keep money as simple as possible. I detail seven of those steps in this book, *Money Well Saved*. And the more you come to manage your income *and* spending in alignment with those steps, the greater financial peace of mind you will experience in your life.

Pray to God but continue rowing to shore.

—Russian proverb

STEP ONE

Spend With a Purpose

Chapter One

Like Beads for Manhattan

The great thing in this world is not so much where we are but in what direction we are moving.

—Oliver Wendell Holmes

We learned in school how the first settlers of the island that is now known as Manhattan traded what has become the most valuable piece of real estate on the planet for nothing more than a few flashy trinkets. Like beads for Manhattan, a lot of our spending accomplishes nothing more than robbing us of our potential to build financial security and the peace of mind that goes with it.

Of course, we all have real expenses and the reason we work is to support our lifestyle. However, almost all of us indulge in a little or a lot of absolutely unnecessary and, even, wasteful spending. And by reducing or, even, eliminating unnecessary and wasteful spending much of your potential can be recaptured.

How many times have you taken money out of the ATM and two or three days later it's gone and you can't remember where? Too many of us spend too much money in this sort of unconscious state. Money enters and leaves our life as if it had intentions of its own.

Why do we allow this to happen? Often it is simply because we spend without giving it much thought. We are in a store when something, some trinket or another, catches our eye and out comes the plastic.

And spending like that often takes place without any consideration as to whether or not we really need what it is we are buying, whether or not the purchase is in our own best interest, or if we can even afford it! It is almost as if spending has become a reflex action triggered by some impulse beyond our control.

But it is possible to spend *thoughtfully* and with more awareness. In fact, it is absolutely necessary to do so if you are ever to capture the full potential of your income. But that higher level of awareness can only take place when you spend with a purpose—when you spend within the context of what you plan to achieve.

Thoughtful spending dictates that you have a plan for every dollar that enters your life. Without a plan it is all too easy for money to simply slip through our fingers, unaccounted for.

Your goals are what enable you to manage your money within the context of what you aim to achieve. Without goals, your spending is simply without direction. The Seven Steps are, in fact, seven individual financial goals that, together, are the foundation of how money is thoughtfully managed.

And, when you decide that moving towards financial peace of mind is a priority for you, you are able to consider how your spending, and I mean each and every individual instance of spending, is moving you either away from or in the direction of that goal.

Henry David Thoreau, author of the seminal text on simple living, *Walden*, wrote of the examined life. An examined life is a life lived consciously and deliberately in concert with thoughtfully conceived values. It is that same level of consciousness that we seek to bring to our spending. Call it considered spending, or thoughtful spending, whatever, it is spending with an awareness of the transaction that is actually taking place.

And the goal of this new level of conscious spending is to marshal our resources so that we not surrender our potential and, like beads for Manhattan, that we not exchange our blessings for baubles.

Chapter Two

The Dickens You Say

Annual income twenty pounds, annual
expenditures nineteen six, result happiness.
Annual income twenty pounds, annual
expenditures twenty pounds ought and six, result
misery.

—from *David Copperfield*

Spending more than you earn is a recipe for financial disaster. That is as true now as it was back in the days of Charles Dickens. The foundation of financial peace of mind, on the other hand, is to live *comfortably* within your income.

The amount of financial peace of mind you enjoy depends, largely, on how financially secure you feel. So, if you are living too close to the financial edge, if your debts are keeping you awake at night or you're living paycheck to paycheck, then you will never enjoy a sense of serenity about your finances.

The future also plays a role in how much financial peace of mind you experience in the present. The more secure you feel about your financial future, the greater your financial peace of mind will be in the here and now.

But one common cause of financial stress these days is the sense of dread many of us live with because we know our financial future is going unaccounted for. Most of us know we should be saving more, even if few of us know exactly how much more it should be. We all know, too, that, even if we had the option of working forever, few of us will actually want to do so.

Still, with all the more immediate demands on our income, saving any amount at all, much less enough so that one day you have the option of kissing the rat-race goodbye, seems almost impossible. So, instead, many of us simply ignore the subject altogether, doing not even what little we could out of a sense of hopelessness.

But you can never really fool yourself into a false sense of security and you know when you are ignoring your future. And that knowledge is always there, as I said, a sense of dread that makes it all but impossible to have any real measure of financial peace of mind, at all.

And, so, you are left feeling anxious and powerless and facing an uncertain financial future. I'm sure you can see how this situation is contrary to *ever* achieving financial peace of mind as long as you allow it to continue.

The answer, then, is to face the issue and take steps to secure the financial aspects of not only the present but the future, as well. And by doing so, you will also take great strides towards greater financial peace of mind.

And, yes, you can take one very big step towards securing both today and tomorrow simply by adhering to the most basic of all money management principles—spend less than you earn. Because the only source of the money necessary to secure the present and the future is the money you earn today.

If that sounds patently obvious to you, however, it is a message that is, nevertheless, not reaching the vast majority of us. U. S. Government statistics reveal that these days there are many of us who are actually spending *more* than we earn!

When you spend more than you earn, you are obviously overspending your income. But overspending is not only spending more than you earn, overspending is also when the amount you spend every month is not far enough below your monthly income to provide for sufficient savings.

Many of us fail to take into account that second definition of overspending and, so, we are lulled into a false sense of security about our financial condition. But sooner or later, the truth will become self-evident.

So, how is it possible to spend more than you earn? Well, the most common way to do so is through the use of credit and one of the most common signs of overspending is carrying a balance from month to month on one or more credit cards.

Credit card debt is a huge problem in the USA these days. It is also a major cause of financial stress for many of us. Another common sign of overspending is what's known as living paycheck to paycheck. Living paycheck to paycheck is also another prevalent cause of financial stress.

Living with credit card debt and living paycheck to paycheck can be thought of as living close to the financial edge. One wrong move, the slightest nudge even, might be enough to push you over that edge.

I'm sure you can see how living like that is not conducive to your financial peace of mind. And you can probably understand that the further you are able to back away from that edge, the more you will enhance your financial peace of mind.

The process of stepping back from the edge begins when you commit to spending less than you earn. The next step is to actually begin to spend and *live* in alignment with that commitment.

A commitment can be thought of as a goal and the first step towards achieving the goal of living within your income is to thoughtfully consider each dollar you spend within the context of that goal.

As you begin this process of examining your spending more closely, do not make the mistake of thinking that small amounts of money are not important. It is very important for you to realize that every dollar you earn has the same value and that any amount of money, no matter how small, is an opportunity to reduce your spending.

After all, you can only grow where you are planted but the longer you wait to begin, the later in life you will reach your goals. The best time to begin was before now, the next best time, however, is today.

To live the spirit of the Seven Steps is to treat your blessings with respect. Small amounts or large, *all* the money you earn is a gift that empowers the rest of your life. To spend without regard is to disrespect your blessings and simply contrary to the spirit of the Seven Steps.

Chapter Three

Spending Like Crazy

*A man's life consisteth not in the abundance of
the things he possesseth.*

—from *The Gospel According to Luke*

This first step towards greater financial peace of mind is based on this simple premise: The less you spend of what you earn, the more financial peace of mind you are likely to experience. When it comes to spending, then, less is more.

It is at this point, however, that the real world intrudes. In the world we are living in today the path to greater financial peace of mind is the road less traveled.

The fact is, in the USA and many other developed nations around the world, we live in a society where spending like crazy is the norm. That being the case, when an individual elects to make financial peace of mind a priority in his or her life, they will be stepping outside the mainstream. But, when spending like crazy is accepted as perfectly rational behavior, spending otherwise will often be considered irrational.

But it is not spending that is the cause of money problems. The problem is spending like crazy, spending you can't really afford—overspending. After all, some of what we earn we need to spend to provide for the necessities and in support of our lifestyle and financial goals. But we are all aware of the troubles that usually come with overspending.

Managing your personal finances to avoid those problems is practically considered an alternative lifestyle these days. If you don't spend every dime you make and then some it's viewed as un-American or something. And, because that is the financial reality in which we live, the road to financial peace of mind can get lonely sometimes simply because it is so at odds with how most people manage their personal finances and live their lives these days.

And the road will definitely have its ups and downs, as the temptation will be great to abandon your quest for financial peace of mind for the more immediate pleasures (if however short-lived) of unbridled spending.

The road to greater financial peace of mind is about making choices that are often contrary to what's going on around you. Money is a finite commodity in our lives and, so, it is required that we allocate our resources, one way or another. That process of allocation requires that we decide among the choices with which we are presented.

On one hand is financial peace of mind while on the other is whole host of spending choices that can lead to credit card debt, living paycheck to paycheck, and all the other ills of overspending including personal bankruptcy, home foreclosure, and even divorce.

First of all, let's reflect on just how fortunate we are to be in the position to choose how we will manage the resources with which we are blessed. We are an incredibly wealthy nation and those of us living in the middle-class of America, as defined by income, live in absolute, not relative, luxury. You might not feel rich but you are rich, if not in fact, then, in potential.

But if you don't feel rich, it is no surprise. Even the upper reaches of middle-class income are strapped by the financial demands of maintaining a middle-class lifestyle. Most of these *demands*, however, are perceived and not actual.

The actual demands on our income are, *actually*, not many. It is our perceived demands, and the costs associated with the level of consumption that they represent, that is where the limits of our income pinch.

The foundation of financial peace of mind is that amount of your income that exceeds your monthly expenses and other spending. The size of the margin by which your income does exceed your spending is one of your most important financial indicators and, as you will learn, it is your margin that will enable your journey towards greater financial peace of mind and empower the remainder of the Seven Steps.

But it is not enough to simply have any amount of breathing room between what you earn and what you spend. The real secret is to manage your finances so that your margin is steadily growing, larger and larger, over time. The larger your margin, the greater financial peace of mind you will enjoy and that is why I refer to that amount by which your income exceeds your spending as a *margin of peace.*

In the chapters that follow, you will learn how to grow your margin even if you never spend less than you are spending today! And, as your margin grows, the percentage of your income that goes to spending will get smaller and smaller and you will be able to save more and more.

How much should you be saving? There is no definitive answer to that question but the key to financial peace of mind is that the amount you save, month after month and year after year, should be growing. So, the goal is simply to save more.

If you think about it, achieving a goal is like taking a journey. Whenever you begin a journey, it will help to have a map. In order for a map to do you any good, however, you first need at least two pieces of information—where you are and where you are going.

If we think of the starting point as Point A and your destination as Point B, each of your financial goals represents a destination of sorts, an individual Point B. But the road ahead is defined as much by the place from which you start as the place you plan to end. So, now, we will proceed to define Point A.

Chapter Four

Where Am I?

He that will not be counseled cannot be helped.

—Benjamin Franklin

The first step in the process of establishing your present financial condition is to determine how much of a margin you now have, if any, between what you earn and what you spend every month. In order to arrive at that figure, all you do is simply subtract the total of your monthly spending from the total of your monthly income.

Sounds easy enough, right? Well, in fact, it is not easy because it is not *that* simple. Certainly, you know what bills you pay every month but if you think of your money-life as a bucket into which you pour your monthly income, your monthly bills are just one hole in that bucket through which money drains out—but there are more, aren't there? Yes, there are, including some that you probably don't even realize exist!

When a business projects and documents its monthly income and expenses, that document is called a *Monthly Income and Expense Statement.* Although the business model of this document does not apply exactly to your personal finances, you should, likewise, document your *projected* income and expenses at the beginning of each month. Why? Because going through the process of doing so will force you to think about your finances in a meaningful way. And, for some of you, it might well be the first time you take a hard look at where your money is going!

To document your monthly income and expenses you will prepare a *personal* Monthly Income and Expenses Statement or, simply, IES, for short. As I stated, arriving at your bottom line is a more complex proposition than you probably imagine at this point, but for now, let's just get some numbers down on paper.

To begin, all you will need is a sheet of lined notebook paper and a pencil. Draw a line down the middle of the sheet (from top to bottom); doing so will give you two columns. Now, at the top of the left-hand column write "Monthly Income" and at the top of the right-hand column write "Monthly Expenditures."

The first number you will enter, on the income side of the ledger (*ledger* is just the common term for a paper with columns in which numbers are listed), will be your monthly *gross* income. Your *gross* income is what you earn before income and employment taxes are deducted. Your *net* income, on the other hand, is the amount you actually see on your check, what most of us refer to as our *take-home pay*.

Then, in the expenses column and using your pay stub as a reference, you list the individual amounts deducted for income and employment taxes. Next you subtract the total of those deductions from your gross income to arrive at your monthly *net* income and the result should look something like this:

Monthly Income ($)		Monthly Expenditures ($)	
Gross Income	3,000		
		Federal Tax	300
		State Tax	75
		OASDI	186
		Medicare	43.50
Net Income	2,395.50		

If your monthly gross income is the same from month to month, all you really need to do is write down the monthly total, even if you are paid more than once a month. If your income varies from month to month, you will need to arrive at a monthly average to enter; for the purposes of this exercise, an estimate will work just fine.

Now, we continue in the expenditures side of the ledger and, at this point, I want to define a few of the terms I will be using so we are both on the same page, so to speak:

Not all spending is exactly the same and the differences must be accounted for in your IES. For example, there are living *expenses* and there is *debt*. The biggest difference between an expense and a debt is that a debt can be paid off. An expense, on the other hand, cannot be paid off because it is more like a recurring cost of living. A car payment is a debt, while the electric bill is an expense.

That will be the criteria by which you will categorize each of your regular bills when completing your IES—as either a debt or an expense. But your bills are different in other ways, as well, and you should consider the implications of those differences on how you manage your money. For example, the monthly amount due on each of your bills is either *fixed* or *variable*.

A bill is *fixed* if the amount due is the same every month. Rent is usually the same amount every month and, so, it is one example of a *fixed expense*. A car payment is, likewise, fixed but it is a *debt* not an *expense*.

On the other hand, the amount due on some bills will usually *vary* from month to month. Utility bills, for example, are usually for a different amount every month. Any bill that does not have a payment amount that is fixed, then, is *variable*.

There are two methods for accounting for recurring, variable spending in your IES. One is simply to enter an amount equal to the highest amount the bill has been in the past twelve months. This will require you to research your receipts to arrive at that figure.

Another way to account for a recurring, variable monthly expense in your IES is to budget a monthly amount equal to the *average* monthly bill over the past year. This method is more advanced than the other, however, and will usually require some tweaking when you begin using it; more on this method, later in the book.

Sometimes, in addition to fixed or variable, people also think of spending as either *discretionary* or *non-discretionary*. In general, we tend to think of a debt or expense as non-discretionary if there is certain to be some fairly immediate and negative consequence if it is not paid.

For example, most of us would consider our rent or mortgage payment as non-discretionary because, if you don't pay the bill, you will find yourself out in the street. Same thing when it comes to your car payment—don't pay it and you *will* wind up walking!

Discretionary spending, on the other hand, is spending over which you have some *discretion* or control such as dining out or entertainment expenses such as cable television or movie rentals. And there are no serious consequences if you choose to not spend those *discretionary* dollars.

But, the fact is, I would consider almost every dollar you spend as discretionary, particularly if you are living way too close to the financial edge. Take the two examples of non-discretionary spending I just mentioned: rent and mortgage payments. You might think that rent is a fixed, non-discretionary expense but, in fact, you do have options.

For example, you *could* get a roommate, move to some place cheaper, or you could even take advantage of some rent-free option that might be available to you (like I did with my brother, Jack). A mortgage, likewise, is usually accepted as fixed and non-discretionary when, in fact, there are steps you could take to save money to include selling the house and moving into a lower cost apartment.

There are, of course, many other options in each situation. Those I mentioned are only examples, not suggestions, and they are only intended to get you thinking about how most expenses are, actually, discretionary to one extent or another. We always enjoy some measure of choice when it comes to spending!

Some variable monthly *expenses*, however, are not so easy to classify as either discretionary or non-discretionary because they often contain elements of both kinds of spending. Money spent on groceries, for example, can include both discretionary and non-discretionary spending.

After you have arrived at your net income, you next list each of your *debts* on its own line in the "Expenditures" column. Do not list *expenses* yet, and keep the difference between debts and expenses in mind as you complete your IES. The most common debts are items such as your mortgage and car payment and the amount you spend every month on your revolving debt such as credit card bills. For example:

Monthly Income ($)		Monthly Expenditures ($)	
Gross Income	3,000		
		Federal Tax	300
		State Tax	75
		OASDI	186
		Medicare	43.50
Net Income	2,395.50		
		Mortgage	900
		Car Loan	250
		MasterCard	65
		Visa	35
		Debt Total	1,250

When you divide the total of your monthly debt payments by the amount of your monthly *gross* (not *net!*) income, the resultant percentage is known as your *debt ratio.* Your debt ratio is an important number to you because it is a very important number to any *reputable* lender. If, for example, you want to buy a house, it is the standard practice in the banking industry that the monthly payments on a mortgage not exceed twenty-eight percent of your gross income.

But lenders will also take your other debts into consideration, as well, and will generally limit the total of your debt payments—mortgage payment plus other debts—to thirty-six percent of your gross income. What that means to you is that every percentage point by which your non-mortgage debt exceeds eight percent of your gross income, the amount you can borrow to buy a house will be reduced by that same one percent. In other words, more debt equals less house!

The next step in completing your monthly IES is to first list each of your recurring monthly *expenses* such as rent, groceries, gas, and utility bills. Then, next to each, write either an estimate of the monthly average amount if the expense is variable or the actual amount if it is fixed. Now you add the total of your debts and expenses and subtract that amount from the total of your monthly net income.

Monthly Income ($)		Monthly Expenditures ($)	
Net Income	2,395.50 (a)		
		Mortgage	900
		Car Loan	250
		MasterCard	65
		Visa	35
		Debt Total	1,250 (b)
		Groceries	250
		Gas/Car	150
		Car Insurance	85
		Cell Phone	65
		Total Expenses	550 (c)
		Total (b+c):	1,800 (d)
		Margin (a−d):	595.50

Don't forget to include the monthly allotment necessary to cover any debt or expense you might have that comes due on some schedule other than monthly. For example, let's say you are billed $600 every six months for automobile insurance (an expense). You will divide the amount by the number of months to arrive at the figure you will write down as the monthly cost (in this example, $600/6 = $100).

If, later on, you want a prepared format on which to enter your figures, or want to see what a sample IES looks like, simply search the internet using the phrase *personal* income and expense statement or something similar. (If you exclude the word "personal" when you search, you are likely to get a version of the form intended for use by a business.)

Fill-in-the-blanks type forms and completed samples of this document are available at many of the popular financial websites, as well. Now, eventually, you might want to run your finances using one of the popular financial software programs. Those programs can generate more information, more readily, than you can otherwise. But for now, tackling this project manually is probably enough of a challenge.

Anyway, once you have arrived at your bottom line, the next step is to consider what that number means to you. If, at this point, your monthly spending already adds up to more than your monthly income, you are in a serious financial bind because you are definitely overspending. This also means that you are being forced to make up the difference somehow.

Chances are, if you are like most people who overspend, that difference is going on one credit card or another. Remember—the most common sign of overspending is carrying a balance on one or more credit cards from month to month. But, even if your numbers show that you are not overspending or, even, if your monthly spending adds up to less than your income and you already *seem* to have some margin, the question is: Oh, really?

Chapter Five

The Spending Diary

*Whatever you can do, or dream you can, begin
it...boldness has genius, power, and magic in it!*

—Goethe

Before you answer that question, let me give you a few
more issues to consider. One is that if your expenses and income
are about the same, you are in that condition known as living
paycheck-to-paycheck. That means your financial security is
very tenuous and you need to take steps to *thoughtfully* back
away from the financial edge as soon as possible—especially if
you have little or no savings!

Also, even if your expenses are less than your income,
you need to ask yourself how much less because any amount less
than ten percent means you are probably not saving enough for
the future. And, if you're not securing your future, you will
never enjoy any true measure of financial peace of mind.

OK, so how about if your margin is ten percent, that, seemingly, magical figure that many money gurus recommend you *should* be saving? Well, although there are some people who would be thrilled to have a margin of ten percent, the truth is that spending ninety percent of what you earn is still living way too close to the financial edge.

The *problem* with a ten percent margin is that it does not really equal much in the way of financial cushion. For example, take a monthly income of $3,000.

Now, $3,000 a month might seem like a lot or a little to you, personally, but the reality is that ten percent of that, $300, just does not go very far these days. I mean, $300 won't cover most emergency dental bills or even buy a set of tires. And if you don't have any savings to fall back on, you will probably wind up going into debt to pay the tab.

"That's true," you might be thinking, "but I could use the $300 to pay off the balance in fairly short order." The problem with that conclusion is that these kinds of financial *surprises* sneak up on us all too often. An unfortunate string of them and, all of the sudden, you're in hock up to your eyeballs!

You see, most of us fail to adequately account for all of our actual expenses. So, when (not *if*) an expense comes up for which you did not account, you will need to turn to your margin to cover those kinds of expenses. But, if your margin is insufficient to do so, you most likely will be forced to resort to debt to cover the shortfall.

Even if your income places you solidly in the middle class, a margin of twenty-percent is not really all that much in terms of absolute purchasing power. But, as important as the size of your margin is, what is even more important, as I have already written, is that it is steadily growing over time. And the way you will track the growth of your margin, and the way you will heighten your level of financial awareness, will be by completing a new IES at the beginning of each month. (Although your IES will soon morph into another document, altogether!)

With many of my clients, the simple act of documenting their spending using an Income and Expense Statement is often the first step to a process of becoming enlightened about their spending. There is more to the process than this single step, but it is a crucial first step in their journey towards greater financial peace of mind.

Now, with your IES in hand, comes the next step: To think about how you can increase your margin by reducing or eliminating any of your regular monthly expenditures.

It is my experience that almost all of us have some amount of fat in our spending. In fact, I would estimate that most of us can reduce our spending somewhere between five and twenty-five percent without it having much, if any, of a negative impact on the quality of our lives.

This is the case because almost all of us do, in fact, regularly engage in some spending that could be considered unnecessary, if not out and out wasteful as well!

Once you have the first draft of your IES completed, you can see if any of your regular expenditures fall into either the unnecessary or wasteful category of spending. This might well be the case but, if not, there is a tool you can use to dig a whole lot deeper into your spending. The numbers revealed in your monthly IES are not much more than a place to start, but to more fully empower your financial awareness will require that you keep, what I call, a *spending diary*.

A spending diary is simply a daily log of what you have spent your money on that day. And, as simple as it sounds, there is a sort of money magic about keeping a spending diary. It will be like shining a bright light on your spending. It will allow you to really examine the flow of money *out* of your life. And, for many of you, it could well be the first time you will ever look this closely at your spending.

The most common excuse I hear when it comes to keeping a spending diary is that it is *so* inconvenient. That is just that—an excuse. It might take five minutes every evening but what people really want to avoid is committing their spending to numbers on a page.

Don't worry about keeping your diary in any particular format. Just make your entries daily in whatever format works for you. You should also enter the total of each day's entries, as well, as doing so will enable you to more readily discern your personal spending patterns.

When you keep a spending diary it is hard to ignore the facts. Unnecessary spending will be easier to pinpoint and wasteful spending will stick out like the proverbial sore thumb.

That is the power of a spending diary—it gives you the information you need to begin making better financial decisions by knowing exactly where your money is going!

And, when you know that each and every purchase you make will go down in black and white, it makes you stop and think at the moment of truth: "How will this expense look in my spending diary?"

It might not stop you from making a purchase each and every time, that is not what it is intended to do, but it will make you stop and think at the moment of truth and that *is* what it is intended to do.

After a full calendar month of income and bill paying and of keeping your spending diary, it will be time to sit down and carefully, thoughtfully, and *honestly* examine your spending with a determination to cut out any and all unnecessary and wasteful spending.

It is at this point that you begin to look for opportunities to redirect spending to savings. At first, what you will be looking for is spending that falls into the category of being like beads for Manhattan. Some of the most common expenditures in this category would include calling features on your telephone service, premium cable channels, designer clothes, some groceries, and name-brand over-the-counter medicines.

Those are just a few generic examples, but we all have our own unique opportunities. Some of us buy DVDs that we watch only once or twice while some of us continue to buy shoes or clothes long after our closet is full to bursting.

Do you really need a name-brand aspirin when the generic will save you a dollar a bottle? It's your life, it's your money, and it's your decision to make in each instance. And the way you turn your money-life around and make your way down the road towards greater financial peace of mind is one save-instead-of-spend decision at a time.

Once you have earmarked opportunities along this line, the secret, then, is to actually get that money into savings; otherwise the money will seemingly vanish into other spending and you will not make any progress.

Chapter Six

Money Wise

If you don't know where you're going, you'll probably end up somewhere else.

—David Campbell, Ph.D.

Whenever your spending diary reveals an expense that you can turn into savings, the trick, as I wrote, is to actually get that money moved into savings. The only way to do that is to have a way to allocate your money to specific uses. The best way to accomplish that is to establish a monthly budget.

A budget is one of the basic tools of personal financial management. It is simply a plan for how you will allocate your income and the device for doing so. No business would expect to be able to manage their finances without a budget and neither should you.

Remember I said that you need to have a plan for every dollar you earn? Well, a budget is that plan. It takes the concept of money flowing into and out of your life and allows you to *see* it in black and white right before your eyes. Most importantly, by using a budget, you can actually exert a large measure of control over that flow.

If you don't presently use a monthly budget to manage your income, all I can tell you is that it will be difficult if not impossible to achieve your full financial potential without one. And, if you are sweating just thinking about putting a budget together, guess what? The IES you just completed is, basically, your present monthly budget.

If you want a prepared format on which to enter your figures, search the internet for *monthly budget form* or some similar phrase. Fill-in-the-blanks type forms and sample budgets are available at many of the popular financial websites, as well. But, just as is the case when preparing your monthly IES, it is more important that you get the numbers right and that nothing is overlooked than it is what it looks like.

And that is where budgeting can get tricky. People often try budgeting for a few months only to give up in frustration when the numbers don't add up. The number one reason that budgets fail in that way is because the person trying to budget has failed to account for all of his or her actual spending.

Certainly, our *fixed* debts are easy to account for in a budget. And we are unlikely to simply forget to include our *variable* debts in our budget since we will usually receive a bill when they are due, as well. (Credit card bills, for example.) So, yes, you *can* choose to ignore your debts, and, even, make a conscious decision to not pay them, but it is difficult to forget them altogether!

However, we do not get a bill for most of our monthly *expenses*. And, so, it is not only entirely possible to forget to include them in our budget, especially when we are first learning to budget, it is also real easy to underestimate how much we are actually spending in those expense categories (such as dining out or groceries) that are either discretionary or variable—or both!

But, unless you track your spending in any particular category, how will you know how much you are *actually* spending? If a budget is only off a little in two or three expense categories, then, in total, it could be *way* off!

It is my experience, in working with clients and students, that someone new to the budgeting process will almost invariably underestimate how much they are spending in many, if not all, of the discretionary expenses in their budgets. That is why it is so important that a budget be used in conjunction with a spending diary!

Another reason that budgets fail is that many of your actual expenses are *hidden*. By that, I mean that you are, in a sense, "running a tab" on some of your living expenses. These expenses, though, don't cost you anything until the tab comes due—more on this subject later in the book.

Keep a spending diary and you will know, for a fact, how much you have spent in any individual expense category in your budget in the past month and you will have a *realistic* number to plug into your budget next month—that alone will make it more likely that your effort to budget will succeed. A spending diary will also help you identify the hidden costs I just mentioned.

But at least a few of the numbers in your budget represent a monthly target and, so, what you really need is a way to manage your money in real time, in the present, as the money gets spent.

Chapter Seven

How to Build a Margin

Knowing what your goal is and deciding to
reach it does not necessarily bring you any
closer to it—doing something does.

—George Eld

Regardless of how much you spent in any discretionary expense category last month (such as dining out or entertainment), you *can*, absolutely, choose to spend less in that category next month. Then, all you will need is the discipline to stick to that budgeted amount and a way to track the remaining balance in that category as the month progresses.

When you are able to tell, at a glance, how much of the budgeted amount remains at any time during the month, you will be better able to avoid going over the budgeted amount. This tool to track your spending this way is called a *spending plan*.

A spending plan is a separate piece of your monthly budget and it works similar to a checkbook register. You begin with a certain amount allocated to each *variable expense* category in your spending plan and, each time you spend some amount in any category, you deduct that amount from the balance in that respective account.

For example, let's say you decide to spend $250 on groceries in the coming month. That is the amount you would enter in your spending plan as the beginning balance for the month. Then, each time you spend any money on groceries, you deduct the amount spent from the existing balance to arrive at your remaining balance.

Again, as you can see from that example, a spending plan works like a checkbook register to show you how much money is left in your "account." In that way, you can tell at a glance how much you have available in any particular category. As you get towards the end of the month, you then have the information you need to avoid spending more than you planned.

A spending plan will usually include individual categories for each of your *variable monthly expenses* such as groceries, gas, toiletries, dining out, entertainment, and miscellaneous. You need to be careful about that "miscellaneous" category, though, because it can become a sort of catch-all in which to hide some unpleasant spending secrets.

The category of your spending plan that is the key to this entire process, however, is your *margin account*. Your margin account represents money you plan to not spend. You might prefer to think of the money in your margin account as savings, and it is, but as the monthly amount dedicated to your margin account grows, it will represent your growing financial security, as well.

Once you have prepared your monthly IES, you will see how much income is not already accounted for, if any. If you do have some discretionary income, now is the time to decide what amount of it will be designated as the monthly allotment to your margin account.

It might well be, however, that, when you first begin the budgeting process, you will have no money "left-over" to fund your margin account. That is when your spending diary will begin to pay off—now you have an accounting of exactly where your money is going and the information necessary to decide where you can make cuts in the coming month.

The spending diary, when combined with the power of a spending plan, gives you the information and tools you need to pay yourself first by choosing to reduce or eliminate some spending in order to save, instead.

At the end of each month, you examine your spending and, if you decide to lower the allocated amount in any spending plan category, you raise the amount in your margin account by that same amount. In that way, the money is accounted for at the beginning of the month and will not just be *absorbed* by other spending.

Then, each time you are paid, you pay yourself first by writing a check to your margin (savings) account for whatever amount is allocated to that account from that paycheck. Before you pay any bills, before you spend a dime, you pay yourself first—no other act is more important to your present or future financial peace of mind!

Let's say you decide to switch to generic aspirin from the name-brand you usually buy and that by doing so you save one-dollar a month in your *toiletries* category. You would then lower the amount for that category by that one dollar and add it to the total of your *margin* category. One dollar is not much, I know, but it is a start and another step in the direction of your goal. For that reason, every dollar is important!

For example, a simple step you can take that will get you moving in the right direction would be to simply stop drinking anything but tap water. By doing so, you will be able to move all you used to spend on assorted beverages (which will be easy to determine using your spending diary) and fatten up your margin instead of your waistline.

In your present spending there are probably dozens of other opportunities like those mentioned and all of them can be redirected to, and are better invested in, building your margin. What you will need to do is weed each of them out.

In fact, "weeding" is my term for the process of combing through your spending diary looking for these opportunities and it is a good analogy for what you will be doing because unnecessary or wasteful spending is to sound money management what weeds are to a garden.

All you need to keep a spending plan is a sheet of lined paper with an individual column for each of your categories. If you have more than four categories, you might need two sheets of paper. For my own spending plan, I use a form I put together using the table function in my word processing program, but I make the entries by hand and in pencil so I can easily make any necessary corrections. A spreadsheet program would also work for this purpose if you want to go that route.

I print my blank spending plan forms out on my home printer on regular 8 ½" x 11" sized paper. The forms, themselves, I keep in a three-ring binder using page dividers to keep the pages for each month separated.

At the top of each column of my spending plan, I enter the amount I plan to spend in that category for the month. As the month proceeds, I deduct the amount of any purchase from its respective total. I also note the date of the purchase and the method of payment. I have learned that keeping receipts is the best way to remember the numbers correctly when I am making entries into my spending plan.

(Those receipts I save in a regular letter-sized envelope with the name of the month written on it. These envelopes of monthly receipts I then keep for at least a year. That way, if the need for any particular receipt comes up, I know exactly where to look.)

If you want a prepared spending plan format, or want to view some sample spending plans, simply do an internet search on the words, *spending plan.*

As you begin to build your margin of peace, the question becomes what to do with the money that is freed up by doing so. At first, your margin might only be one or two percent of your income, but what is important and empowering is simply that you begin and that you spend in context and in keeping with the goal of continuing to grow it.

The best place to invest your margin is in yourself—your financial security, your future, your peace of mind, and your dreams. Much of the rest of the book is about how to invest towards those very ends.

And what you must always remember is that the money in your margin account is a resource you do not obligate to spending in any fashion. This is money that serves as a cushion between what you earn and what you spend. Your margin of peace is a true measure of financial comfort.

After a while, you will get better at both keeping a spending diary and working with a spending plan. Also, it is likely that a spending plan based on only one month of spending will need some adjustment as you compile more and better data, over time, about where your money is going.

In fact, your monthly budget will prove to be a living document and a record, of sorts, of your financial development. I recommend that you save copies of your past monthly budgets and spending plan and spending diary pages as they will provide you with a compelling history of your journey towards financial peace of mind.

Little by little, and sometimes by more than a little, in this way you will begin to grow your margin of peace. But the real secret to growing your margin is to control the growth of your spending.

STEP ONE

Part Two

Chapter Eight

The Picture of Wealth

*It is our commitments that give meaning and
purpose to our lives.*

—Frank Rhodes, President, Cornell University,
1990

I want to stress that this is not another get-rich-quick book. If anything, it is something of an unintended primer on how to build wealth slowly. I say that only because the natural outcome of managing your finances according to the Seven Steps will be to grow your savings and investments and, given enough time, your bottom line could grow to be quite substantial.

So, let's go into the subject of building wealth a little more and how it relates to what this book is *actually* about—financial peace of mind.

If you stop and think about it, you will realize that there are only three classes of wealth—unearned, entrepreneurial, and investment. Unearned wealth is money that is, pretty much, handed to you. Two examples of unearned wealth are winning the lottery or being the beneficiary of an inheritance or some other windfall.

Only you know what your chances of inherited wealth are, but I can tell you what your chances of hitting the lottery are—about several million to one or worse—about the same as mine and I don't even play the lottery!

Entrepreneurial wealth, starting a business and making it big, is almost as sizable a gamble as the lottery only the ante is generally higher. In most instances, when you start a business all you are doing is buying a job with longer hours. And businesses fail at an alarming rate.

But many self-made millionaires are business owners. It was not, however the business, itself, that actually made them rich but simply the fact that owning a business does allow a sufficiently motivated individual to harness a few dynamics unique to that setting to earn more than they might as an employee.

The third class of wealth, achieved by the accumulation of assets over time, is what I call *investment* wealth. The only source of the money to fund your investments is your income. So, although it might be called investment wealth, it is actually wealth built on a foundation of saving—money that you earn but do not spend.

Thomas J. Stanley and William D. Danko, the authors of the book *The Millionaire Next Door*, make the point that many of those individuals who have reached millionaire status on a middle-class income did so largely through saving a significant portion of their income. In other words, they did it the old-fashioned way—they earned it!

The way that most of them were able to save so much was to keep their cost of living relatively fixed as their income increased over time. It might seem like a simple plan for growing wealth but there it is and it reflects exactly the goal to continually grow your margin of peace.

Now, that is not to imply that all wealthy people enjoy financial peace of mind. Money comes with its own problems. It happens all the time that people with large incomes go bankrupt. That is because earning money takes a different set of skills than does managing your money wisely to secure your financial future and achieve financial peace of mind. Even the wealthy could benefit from living the Seven Steps.

Investment wealth is something that is *achieved* over time and through hard work and discipline. But the culture of consumerism that is so prevalent these days has led many people to believe that wealth is something to be *perceived.*

People, often mistakenly, judge the financial condition of others by what they see. But real financial success is not efficiently judged by looking at an individual's level of consumption. An extravagant lifestyle, a luxury car, or a Rolex watch can prove false indicators. If you want to know someone's actual financial state, look at his or her balance sheet.

A balance sheet is simply an accounting of someone's assets and liabilities. An asset is any tangible item of value that you own such as the equity in your home or vehicles and including the value of your savings and investments. A liability is basically any debt you have. When you subtract your liabilities from assets, the bottom line represents your *net worth.*

For example, let's say your home is worth $200,000 but that the balance of the mortgage on it is only $150,000. The net worth of that asset, your home, is its value minus the debt owed on it or $50,000.

Now, the ultimate goal of your financial planning does not necessarily need to be a million dollar net worth. And the bottom line is not actually the most revealing figure on a balance sheet. A better indicator of someone's financial condition is the annual growth in their net worth as a percentage of income. What that number reveals is just how closely a person is living to the limits of their income and how much of what they earn they are managing to keep.

The fact is, consumable items, such as cars and jewelry, will usually subtract from an individual's net worth. This is because those kinds of consumer goods, the kind that steadily lose value over time, do not add as much to the asset side of the ledger as they cost you on the liability side.

Every time you make a purchase, you are buying something that will either *appreciate*, that is, go up in value, or *depreciate*, go down in value. Investments are made with the hope that they will appreciate but it doesn't always happen that way.

Any item you consume can be considered to depreciate from the moment it is purchased. Food and clothes are just two examples of depreciating, consumable assets. Cars, too, begin to depreciate as soon as they are purchased. The value of a new car, in particular, drops like a rock as soon as you drive it off the dealer's lot.

Every time you buy a new car, your net worth takes a serious hit. Let's say your net worth is $100,000 and you, feeling flush, decide it's time for a new ride. Being the prudent consumer that you are, you don't over reach and, instead, you opt for a more modestly priced mid-level sedan with a price tag of *only* $22,000.

You pay $5,000 down and finance the rest over five years. What is your net worth after this transaction? It will be less by ten to twenty-five percent of the cost of the car plus tax and license. The point of saving is to grow your net worth but, as you can see, buying depreciating assets accomplishes just the opposite.

Real estate, the home you live in, in particular, is one of the few items you consume (through the utility of providing you with shelter) but that can, and often does, appreciate in value.

Chapter Nine

The Foundation of Wealth

Endeavor vigorously to increase your property.

—Horace

If you want some insight as to your own progress in building your net worth, simply make a rough calculation of how much you have earned during all the years you have been working to date. Then you divide that figure into the amount of your present net worth.

The number you end up with by doing that calculation represents that percentage of your lifetime earnings you have managed to keep. You can spend your potential today or you can realize your potential tomorrow but you can't have it both ways.

You'll first have to prepare a balance sheet (also known as a *Net Worth Statement*) to complete this exercise, obviously, but that is a good thing because you should know your net worth like you know your home telephone number, it is that important an indicator of your financial condition.

If you want a prepared format on which to figure your net worth, or want to view some sample Net Worth Statements, simply do an internet search on the words, "figuring your net worth," or some similar phrase. Fill-in-the-blanks type forms and samples of completed Net Worth Statements are available at many of the popular financial websites, as well.

Also in the book, *The Millionaire Next Door*, is a handy formula to determine how you are doing in regards to building your net worth. What you do is multiply your age by your present gross income and divide the resultant figure by ten. That amount is, roughly, what your net worth *should* be according to the authors of that book.

For example, an individual who is 50 years of age with an annual gross income of $50,000 *should*, according to the authors, have a net worth of $250,000 [($50,000 x 50)/10].

For the sake of an honest appraisal, when using this formula, you should not include any amount of your assets that were unearned such as by way of an inheritance or any other unearned financial windfall.

After you have run the numbers for yourself, you then compare what you *should* have according to that formula to what you *do* have—your actual net worth. If you have more than the formula amount, you have done better than average, but if you have less the question is what will you do to do better in the future?

Here, I want to remind you that the past is not something to beat yourself up over. Regrets pay little in the way of dividends. The value of the past is to learn how we might have done better. Our past mistakes are only that and nothing more *unless* we learn from them. To honor our experiences, then, we should put them to work for us.

Budgets and spending plans are great tools to run your personal finances on a day-to-day basis and one surprising fact revealed in *The Millionaire Next Door* is just how many of the millionaires profiled continued to manage their household finances using a budget.

Now, obviously, once you have achieved a certain level of financial success, you don't need to keep a budget to manage your money but many millionaires still do.

Why? I think it is because the planning and tracking of expenses and expenditures is how many of these millionaires were able to control their spending in the first place. It was also the source of the information they needed to make good financial decisions. And it was that informed financial decision-making which, over time, empowered their ultimate financial success.

Also over time, the close monitoring of their expenses and spending became something of a habit during their climb up the financial ladder. And, based on the results they achieved, they realized just how well doing so served them and, so, many of them simply continue with it even after it is no longer a financial necessity that they do so.

Any habit, even a bad habit, is often hard to break. A habit that has proven its value, like using a personal budget, is that much harder to simply abandon. Still, what it all comes down to is the decision to save and the fortitude to do so in the age of the hyper-consumer.

"Planning and wealth accumulation are significant correlates even among investors with modest incomes"

—from *The Millionaire Next Door* by Danko and Thomas

That is what the authors of that book concluded after years and years of studying individuals who had managed, basically, to save themselves rich—that those who have done so simply worked their plan to do so. This is true, they found, regardless of the level of income and it has been demonstrated by their own studies in this regard that it is possible to build wealth on even a modest income.

> *"...the overwhelming determinant of the accumulation of wealth at retirement is simply the choice to save."*

—from *Choice, Chance, and Wealth Dispersion at Retirement* by Venti and Wise for the National Bureau of Economic Research.

I don't know how to make it any clearer than that. The foundation of both wealth *and* financial peace of mind is saved income—money you earn but don't spend! And the only way to have income available to save is to spend less than you earn.

Chapter Ten

Money Power

There are a million things in the universe you can have, and there are a million things you can't have. It's no fun facing that, but that is the way things are.

—spoken by Captain Kirk (Star Trek)

If saving is one side of the wealth coin, however, the flip side of that coin is every bit as critical to your financial peace of mind—and that flip side is spending. If you can manage to control your expenses, to the extent that you are able to keep them relatively fixed over a long period of time, increased savings and greater financial peace of mind are sure to follow.

Most of us are probably familiar with the concept of "pay yourself first." That concept dictates that you carve out some fixed percentage of your income to save and that you do so before you carve up the rest in order to meet your expenses.

Paying yourself first is a sound concept as long as you understand how it fits in with the goal of moving towards greater financial peace of mind.

When advocates of *pay yourself first* mention a figure, that figure is usually ten percent. So, let's say that you pick ten percent as the amount you will save from now on. Does that mean, then, that you can afford to spend the ninety percent that is left?

Well, let's consider that question from a different perspective by asking it another way—is ten percent enough? The question, then, is enough for what? Remember, the only money you have to accomplish all your financial goals is that money you earn but don't spend—your savings.

Is ten percent enough to do that? Before you answer that question consider that achieving only the fundamental goal of all financial planning—retirement—is going to require that you save at least ten percent of your income for something like forty (yikes!) years or more. But retirement is not our only financial goal, is it?

There is more to life than just making ends meet and we all have our dreams. But dreams almost all come with a price tag attached, don't they? And the only way to realize our dreams, then, is to save for them.

Whether it's a spring wedding, a cabin in the mountains, or a Harley-Davidson motorcycle to ride off into the sunset, our dreams must be accounted for in our financial planning or the chances are they will never see the light of day.

Taxes already take a bite out of what you earn. This can amount to as much as twenty percent or more of your gross pay. So, between what is left after taxes are deducted, your *net* pay, and however much you are spending, is the all the money you have to both secure your future and finance your dreams.

Whatever your margin amounts to, all the sudden, hardly seems like enough, does it? The truth is that ten percent will not be enough. Ten percent of your gross income will, in fact, prove woefully inadequate.

Another problem with picking some fixed percentage of your income to save is that, although the amount will grow as your income increases, that growth will not realize your full potential to grow your margin even larger and faster.

Finally, the fact that you are paying yourself first can lull you into a false sense of security. Don't get me wrong, acting on your decision to save is the single most important step down the road towards greater financial peace of mind. After all, the best time to plant an Oak tree was twenty years ago but, if you haven't planted one yet, the next best time is now. But as important as is to set aside a portion of your income to save, it is just as important to control your spending.

Remember the strategy employed by those interviewed in *The Millionaire Next Door*—the trick is to keep your expenses relatively fixed as inflation and other factors lift your income over time. By doing so, the margin between what you spend and don't spend will grow, sometimes dramatically, over time.

What most of us do is just the opposite of that—as our income grows, we also grow our expenses so that we never make any real financial progress. We might collect a bunch of toys and a house and garage (and storage unit!) full of so much *stuff*, but our financial security isn't growing to match our potential.

Another problem with growing your expenses right along with your income is the stress it puts on you to maintain that income. If you are living close to the limit of your income and your income is to stop or even just fall too far below your bare living expenses, for any reason, it will almost certainly lead to a financial disaster.

That is why you hear it said that many of us are only a couple of missed paychecks from being homeless. A person who is without sufficient savings and living paycheck to paycheck is without a financial safety net of savings to fall back on in case of a financial emergency.

The only way to build that safety net is through savings, but how can you save if you are spending all you earn? Living paycheck to paycheck is a financial house of cards and, if the money ever stops flowing, the house will come tumbling down.

There are steps you can take and should take to protect yourself in the event that it happens, but the best way to approach the issue is to keep your expenses in check. Obviously, you need to make saving a priority and pay yourself first, but it is also vital to the process that you plan to control the growth of your spending.

Now, let's say that you have no aspirations to achieve a million dollar net worth. And, after all, that is not really the subject of this book. Instead, let's assume that all you're after is to achieve greater financial peace of mind—that all you want is to run your personal finances in such a way that money never becomes, or ceases to be, an issue in your life.

Although it would seem as if the two goals are individual and not related, they do, in fact, go hand in hand. The steps to accomplish either will allow you to accomplish both given enough time to work their simple magic. The means to both ends are the same and those means are spelled out in the Seven Steps.

And the foundation upon which you will build both financial security *and* financial serenity is that amount of your income that you *don't* spend—your margin of peace.

Yes, if you are able to maintain a constant rate of savings as a percentage of your income, the actual dollar amount you are saving will increase with any increase in your income. But imagine if, while realizing those same increases in your income, you were able to keep your expenses *relatively* fixed from now on—that is the secret to both financial security and financial peace of mind!

Chapter Eleven

When Less is More

*Life is like a game of cards. The hand that is
dealt you represents determinism. The way you
play the hand you are dealt? That is free will.*

—Nehru

So, here is the bottom line—the closer you are to spending 100% of what you earn, the less financial security you will have in your life. On the other hand, the lower the percentage of your income that you spend is, the greater your financial security. And, the less you spend of what you earn, the more you will be able to save—that equation is automatic.

The real power of income growth, however, is unleashed when you keep your expenses as constant as possible in absolute dollars. If you are spending $200 a month on groceries today you should strive to be spending $200 a month on groceries ten years from today.

Will that always be practical or possible? Maybe not, but it is only by having that as a goal that you will be able to focus and direct your actions to that specific outcome. That is the power unique to a life lived towards accomplishing established goals.

Yes, I know about inflation and its effect on buying power. And, just as yes, it might not always be possible to keep your spending fixed in all expense categories from now on. But the real power of any individual goal is the way in which it can help us to drive our actions towards our intended target.

Maybe you won't be able to keep your grocery spending constant for the next decade but knowing that you can align your spending with that goal, to the fullest extent practical, will allow you to make informed decisions about how you choose to spend.

And, it also makes you aware that you are in control of your bottom line. If you can't help but increase your spending on groceries or some other category, maybe you can offset that increase in some other more discretionary expense category, say, dining out or entertainment. If so, in that way, you have still managed to meet your bottom line goal of zero net growth in spending.

The more you are able to keep your expenses fixed over time, the more you aren't spending will become, also over time and as your income grows—but only to the extent that you are able to keep your expenses from growing right along with your income.

This point shows the importance of fixing costs whenever it makes sense to do so. A mortgage is a good example of this. One expense we all face is the need for housing. When you secure a fixed mortgage to buy a home, you are *fixing* that cost in your budget. Fixing a cost allows you to plan with more certainty.

If you are like most homebuyers, the amount of your mortgage payment is likely to be equal to about twenty-five percent of your gross income at the time you made the purchase. That figure is based on lender-established ratios having to do with mortgage-debt and income. But, as the years pass, that percentage number will go down simply because your income has gone up.

I remember when I bought my first home. My payment at the time was just about equal to that twenty-five percent figure. Today, the amount of that mortgage payment would not be equal to even one percent of my income!

Can you imagine that? Can you imagine spending only one-percent of you gross income on your mortgage payment? That is a great example of how keeping your expenses fixed over a long period of time can have the same effect as spending less when it comes to freeing up money to save.

But, in the short-term, the quickest way to find the savings that will be the foundation of your margin will be to reduce or eliminate the fat in your budget in order to get yourself some breathing room. Your cash flow statement, monthly budget, spending diary, and spending plan are all great tools to help you do just that.

The next step towards greater financial peace of mind, once you have realized those savings accomplished by taking cuts in your current expenditures, is to put your margin on a path that will keep it growing for as long as you work for a living. The plan to accomplish that is the subject of the next part of this book and it is amazingly simple yet almost unbelievably powerful.

Significant problems we face cannot be solved at the same level of thinking we were at when we created them.

—Albert Einstein

STEP TWO

Plan to Grow

Chapter Twelve

A Plan to Grow

Focusing our attention—daily and hourly—not
on what is wrong, but on what we love and
value, allows us to participate in the birth of a
better future, ushered in by the choices we make
each and every day.

—Carol Pearson

We all are so blessed in so many ways but, sometimes, when living becomes a struggle, we forget how lucky we are just to be alive. Just reminding yourself of that from time to time will go a long way towards helping you keep your perspective and stay positive in the face of everyday events. And, I have found, that it will also help to de-funk your money karma (or, *something*) if you have a way to acknowledge your good fortune.

Most of us are lucky enough to have a job and to earn the money that empowers so many other aspects of living, from keeping the lights on to raising our children. But, when we spend all we earn, as fast as we earn it (and then some in many cases), we fail, I think, to give proper thanks as might be displayed through a more considered marshalling of our resources.

Yes, what we earn is ours, but it has never been the case that it is *all* ours. Uncle Sam takes his cut, then Social Security and Medicare get some, and, then, most states take a portion, as well.

And, then, there is the fact that the future is *out there*, waiting, and needs to be considered in our financial planning. But, when you spend all you earn in support of the present, you do so at the expense of your future financial security. Anxiety related to inadequate savings is weighing heavy on the minds of many of us today.

In the previous chapters, you were introduced to the tools that will help you begin to make better decisions when it comes to how you choose to spend your money. By following the exercises in Step One, you can now consider how you might turn some of your present expenses into savings.

Your spending diary will help to illuminate opportunities to save in your daily spending. These savings, then, can be targeted towards building your margin account and will provide the foundation of that account.

But the foundation upon which you build a better financial future is a commitment to spend less than you earn and to save the difference. Your commitment to saving is the single most powerful and empowering of all financial decisions you will ever make.

The authors of the *Millionaire Next Door* found that the single distinction that separated self-made millionaires from other less financially-successful individuals was not income but the fact that they simply had a plan to save. Think about that! Yes, action is important, but before you can act you need a plan or your actions will be without direction and, so, likely to be *misguided* because they will be *unguided*.

In the book, *Alice's Adventures In Wonderland*, written by Lewis Carroll, the following conversation takes place between Alice and the Cheshire Cat:

> *"Cheshire Puss..." said Alice, "can you tell me please which way I should go from here?"*
>
> *"That depends a good deal on where you want to get to," said the Cat.*
>
> *"I don't much care where," said Alice.*
>
> *"Then it doesn't matter which way you go," said the Cat.*
>
> *"...so long as I get somewhere," added Alice as an explanation.*
>
> *"Oh, you're sure to do that," said the Cat, "if only you walk long enough."*

It is simply not enough in life to want to get *somewhere* because *somewhere* does not provide the information you need to sufficiently plan your journey! Remember the earlier quote from David Campbell—*if you don't know where you're going, you'll probably end up somewhere else.* Everyday you are writing the history of your future. Either you are defining it for yourself or you are choosing to be a minor player in your own life.

If you choose to be the author of your life, you must plan for what you want to achieve. If you do not take that fundamental step, you will definitely end up *somewhere*, but the odds are against it being what you had in mind!

You need to know where you are going in order to plan how you will get there—and that is exactly the function of goal-setting. And, not only will your goals serve to help you plan your life, they will also help you make good decisions. And, in that way, goals are invaluable.

Each goal, you see, serves as a reference point and all your goals together form a sort of matrix. It is that matrix that will let you weigh the relative merit of one course of action versus another.

As this relates to financial planning, your *financial* goals are what provide the context for making sound financial decisions. This point is illustrated in a conversation I once had with a friend of mine.

Jim, who knew I taught personal financial management, told me that he had recently come into some money. He asked me if I thought it would be a good idea if he spent some of that money acquiring a certain vehicle he wanted.

> *"Well," I said, "that depends on how spending that money fits in with achieving your other financial goals."*

> *"What do you mean?" he asked.*

"I mean, to what extent will buying that vehicle empower or impede your ability to reach your other established financial goals?"

Jim skipped a beat, then, replied, "I guess I don't have any financial goals."

"Then you might as well buy what you want," I said, "because in that case you really can't make a bad financial decision."

What I did not say was that there was no way he could make a good decision, either. Like Alice, Jim is sort of just *out there,* wandering around aimlessly on a mad dash through a Wonderland of his own. And, also like Alice, Jim doesn't have a precise destination in mind, so, how can it matter what direction he takes?

Our plans miscarry because they are without direction.

—Seneca

Seneca was a philosopher in ancient Rome, so his message is real, real old and proof positive that there *is* nothing new under the sun. And his message is as true and important today as it was all those hundreds of years ago. In order to achieve financial security, and the peace of mind that comes with it, you must have a plan to do so. Either that or you have chosen to cast your fate to the wind.

I worked for years in a job where every year every employee would receive an annual cost of living raise. Often, employees would discuss their plans for the next raise among each other. I found it sort of fascinating to hear them making plans to spend money they had yet to realize. In fact, many of them would actually go out and finance cars and other purchases based on the assumption that the money was coming!

There was, however, a fly in their ointment. If the raise was announced to be, say, five percent, they would then proceed to figure the amount the raise would be equal to in dollars. The problem was that they did so using, what I can only describe as, a sort of *fuzzy math*. First, they would figure the raise based on their gross income and then they would go on to ignore all taxes and other deductions including the annual increase in health care premiums.

That fuzzy math made it inevitable that they would grossly over-estimate the amount they would actually realize in their paycheck and, yet, year after year, I watched as many of them would actually proceed to spend based on those inflated and absolutely wrong numbers! After only a couple years of applying fuzzy math like that, they couldn't help but fall behind!

As I watched this same scenario play itself out every year, it finally dawned on me that if each raise was, on one hand, an opportunity to *spend* more, it was, on the other hand, an opportunity to *save* more. It was, indeed, something of an *Aha!* moment for me.

I put in place a plan to take advantage of that opportunity and began to save most of each raise I received. Eventually, I was saving over one-half of my net income.

As I watched my own path divert from the more usual path of earn-more-spend-more followed by my fellow employees, it dawned on me that the path towards greater financial peace of mind was simply to take advantage of the golden opportunity we all have to increase our savings each and every time we get a pay raise.

Chapter Thirteen

Accounting for Your Good Fortune

There is no chance, no destiny, no fate, that can
circumvent or hinder or control the firm resolve
of a determined soul.

—Ella Wheeler Wilcox

Financial security is built on a foundation of savings from earned income. So, if you are to achieve financial security, you need a plan to save.

As is the case with any plan, however, you can only go forward from where you are today. Regardless, however, of where you are today, there is a way to save, even if you think it is impossible to reduce your *present* spending at all.

Most of us who are employed receive periodic pay raises. Often, these pay raises are annual and sometimes they are the result of nothing more than time on the job or inflation. Whatever the exact reason, most of us do receive a regular pay raise once a year or so.

But what happens, more often than not, is that our raises seem to vanish—lost in the fog of spending—especially if you don't keep a spending diary or use a budget to manage your finances. I mean, after all, once they take out taxes and what's left gets spread out over the entire year, it's hardly enough to make a difference, right?

Well, it might not make much of a difference in your spending but it can make a *huge* difference in your savings. Let's say you get a five percent raise and you are presently saving ten percent of your income. If you're making $3,000 a month and get paid every other week, a five percent raise will put about $50 more in your pocket each payday. And we all know how easy it will be to spend another fifty bucks, right?

But if you take that raise and add it to what you're presently saving, instead of letting it get lost in your spending, the amount it represents as a percentage of savings can be much more meaningful. If you are presently saving ten percent of your income, continuing with the example above, and you put that same raise into a tax-deferred retirement account, you have just increased your savings by *fifty percent*!

So, no, fifty bucks is not enough to change your lifestyle but it *can* change the way you save in a big way. And, then, there is this—when we let money get lost in the shuffle of spending and getting, we fail, I think, to adequately acknowledge our good fortune.

Every pay raise, large or small, presents a distinct opportunity to increase your savings, even if, today, you are not managing to save anything at all! The trick is to take advantage of that opportunity, somehow. How can you do that? All it takes is that you follow, what I call, *The Fifty Percent Plan*—you simply plan to save at least one-half of every pay raise that you receive from now on.

Presently, you might or might not have any margin between what you earn and what you spend. You might be living paycheck to paycheck or, even worse, your expenses might exceed your income. Whatever the case may be, if you follow this plan, and you save one-half of every raise you get from now on, you will, *absolutely*, grow the size of your margin and increase the amount you are saving—guaranteed!

Let me show you the power of following The Fifty Percent Plan:

Let's say you are presently earning $52,000 a year and that you get paid every two weeks. Now, let's also assume that you get a five percent raise equal to $2,600. In this example, and following The Plan, you would then increase your annual contribution to your margin account by $1,300—one-half of the total amount of the raise. Dividing that amount over the year, it would equal an additional $50 a pay period to savings.

Each time you are paid, then, you will write a check to yourself that now includes this increased amount and deposit it to your savings account. If you do that, then, there is no way that extra income will vanish into everyday spending.

As simple as this strategy might be, and it is very simple indeed, it works like magic given enough time. For example, let's assume that you are presently earning an annual salary of $36,000. Let's also assume that your margin, the amount you are presently saving, is equal to ten percent of your gross income, $3,600.

Now, let's say you receive a five-percent pay raise. That five percent would be equal to $1,800. One-half of that would be $900 and that is the amount you would add to your margin account, raising the annual total of your savings to $4,500.

Whereas you were saving ten percent of your previous gross income, the increased amount, $4,500, equals almost twelve percent of the amount of your increased salary of $37,800.

But do not wait until the end of the year to put that money away or it is almost certain to be gone by then! Instead, divide the annual amount of the raise by the number of times you get paid every year and add that amount to whatever you are presently saving each time you get paid.

Following this plan, if you were to receive another five percent raise a year later, your margin would grow to almost fourteen percent. Although your margin will continue to grow as long as you follow The Plan, even at that early a point, you will be enjoying the benefits of a fourteen percent margin between what you earn and what you spend.

And, every bit as vital to your long-term financial success, your spending will now represent a smaller percentage of your income. Whereas, before, you were spending ninety percent of your income, that percentage has now decreased to eighty-six percent. And, that percentage will continue to go down for as long as you follow The Plan!

Do you see how the plan to save one-half of every pay raise achieves a dramatically different result from a plan to simply save some fixed percentage? If you follow the fixed-percentage plan, and assuming the amount you plan to save is ten percent, your savings will always remain equal to ten percent of your gross pay.

That means that your margin will always be equal to that same ten percent as well—one year from now, two years from now, or five years from now—your margin will be that same ten percent.

To illustrate this point further, because it is very important that you see the potential in The Plan, let's assume your salary increases from $25,000 to $35,000 after a series of five percent annual raises. If you adhere to a plan to save ten percent of your income, your savings will be equal to $3,500 a year when your income reaches $35,000.

If you use The Fifty Percent Plan, instead, you will be saving $7,590 a year when your income reaches that same $35,000 amount—over twice as much! And the total amount saved over the time it takes your income to climb from $25,000 to $35,000 will be dramatically more, as well, by following The Fifty Percent Plan. In fact, your savings will also be more than twice as much when compared to the fixed-percentage plan!

If you are self-employed, this plan will require some modification. Obviously, the self-employed also enjoy increases in income over time through charging higher prices or growing their customer base. If you are self-employed, you, likewise, need a plan to save. Otherwise, the amount of any new earnings is likely to simply disappear into your spending.

The way to avoid that from happening is to increase the amount you budget for your margin account at least once a year and every time you know that you will be realizing an increase in your income.

For example, let's say you project that in the next year the annual revenue of your business will increase by $6,000 and, based on your experience, you estimate that you will net one-half of that, $3,000, as profit.

Now, let's assume that you plan to take all of that $3,000 as a pay raise to yourself. Following The Fifty Percent Plan, you would simply dedicate one-half of that raise to growing your margin account. Every month, then, you would sock away an *additional* $125 to savings.

Again, you need to pay yourself first at the beginning of every month. The first check you write or the first deposit you make at the beginning of every month must be to your margin account. Don't wait until the end of the month after all the bills are paid—pay yourself first! The mechanics are a little different for you if you are self-employed but the end result will be the same.

In fact, if you are self-employed, you often enjoy an even higher degree of control over your income growth. You can choose to expand your business in any number of ways. You have options not available to those of us who work for someone else.

I am certain that you can appreciate the financial benefits and peace of mind that you will enjoy as you experience your margin growing over time. But there is more to it than that! In another part of this book, I will share with you how this single step is the first step to the ultimate in financial peace of mind—financial independence.

Chapter Fourteen

The Vision Thing

In my practice as a psychiatrist, I have found
that helping people to develop personal goals
has proved to be the most effective way to help
them cope with problems.

—Ari Kiev, M.D.

Why do you think goals can prove so beneficial? I think it is because goals give people hope and because, and, perhaps, just as importantly, goals can help to change your focus from the present to the future. In that way, goals empower the act of vision.

When your only focus is on the present it is easy to forget about tomorrow, altogether. By allowing yourself to get lost in the demands and details of daily living, you will often lose sight of the broader perspective that includes the future.

Basking in the present at the expense of the future is not a luxury many of us can afford. And, when you discount your tomorrows in this way, you fail to take advantage of the empowering force that living with a vision can provide you.

A vision can be a powerful force for change in your life. Ultimately, your goals are what define your vision. For example, the goal to have a continually growing margin of peace allows you to imagine yourself actually living in that reality.

But until you define your goals, how will you ever be able to let your imagination go there? Your vision of tomorrow is what makes the future real. So, as soon as you can change your perspective to include the future, a different picture, altogether, comes into view—the *big* picture!

The day to day stuff is still there and needs to be dealt with but by working towards your goals you remove a substantial amount of your present emphasis on who and where you are today. This acts, then, to relieve some of the pressure your present issues are causing you because, now, you can see yourself in better circumstances.

You might be where you are but now, with a more proper emphasis on the future, you can also see where you have the power to go. A vision of the future based on your goals is like a roadmap. Using your cash flow and net worth statements, you now know where you are, and with your vision of the future, you have defined your destination. Now, all that is left is both the hard part and the best part—the journey.

And, remember, who you are today is enough to be who you will be tomorrow.

Do what you can, with what you have, where you are.

—Theodore Roosevelt

Maybe your finances are not in the greatest shape. Maybe today's problems with money are keeping you awake at night. But, sometimes, a light in the distance is hope enough and chance enough.

Hope springs eternal because we have all witnessed how life can change for the better, seemingly overnight. The Seven Steps *can* change your financial life for the better and, if not overnight, they will definitely work their magic over time—all it takes is the motivation to follow them.

You have the power to make your vision of the future a reality by the actions you take and the decisions you make today and then tomorrow, one day after another, and one day at a time.

Chapter Fifteen

Small Steps

The gods help those that help themselves

—Aesop

Change can occur in long jumps or small steps but even small steps can lead to significant progress towards a goal, given enough of them over time. What is important, and what is self-affirming, is that you always strive to keep moving in the right direction in order to keep your momentum going because momentum is a very important consideration when you are just beginning.

There is a law of physics that states that bodies at rest tend to stay at rest while bodies in motion tend to stay in motion. The most difficult part of your journey towards greater financial peace of mind might just be finding the motivation to begin because many long-term goals can simply seem overwhelming.

A better way to approach a large financial goal is to break it up into smaller pieces *and* smaller numbers that you won't have such a hard time dealing with. For example, let's say you plan to retire in thirty years and you have estimated that you will need $500,000 to do so. What works better than focusing on a goal of those dimensions is to think, instead, in terms of thirty individual *and* smaller goals.

If you divide the goal of $500,000 by the thirty years you have to get there and also factor in a presumed interest rate, the task at hand seems much more realistic. And, in that way, it is much more likely that you will be able to muster the motivation to get started.

Your goal at this point, then, is simply to consider how you might reduce your spending using the tools from Step One. Instead of looking at the big picture and years down the road, you should focus on the smaller steps that get you moving and keep you moving in the right direction.

The process of saving more begins with a single small step—the thoughtful consideration of your daily expenditures to look for any possible reductions, no matter how small. Not much to that is there? I mean, you can probably envision yourself doing that, can't you? That is both how you begin and how you begin to build momentum.

But as small and doable a first step as it is, you are, nevertheless, making genuine progress. And it is an important and meaningful part of the process, as well.

You already have the tools you need to begin to write a new future for yourself. You begin, simply, by making a commitment to saving. Then, acting on that decision, you eliminate spending that is not in your own best interest and use those savings as the foundation of your margin of peace. But what will transform your relationship with money is your plan to save one-half of every raise you receive from now on.

The Fifty Percent Plan works like magic for two very good reasons. One is that it does not require any new sacrifice on your part. That is important because it takes a large measure of self-discipline to deny yourself anything over the long term— just ask anyone who has ever been on a diet!

But it's hard to suddenly come up with some new level of self-discipline out of thin air. After all, self-discipline is not something you grow like hair on a Chia Pet! Some of us are born with it and some of us are born, well, missing that gene or something.

That being the case, it is difficult to make any change that will require a measure of self-discipline you do not already possess. Again, The Plan does not require the self-discipline to make any new sacrifices!

And the second reason why The Plan works is that it will not have a negative impact on your present standard of living. Whatever you are spending now, you can keep spending. In fact, if you think about it, the other half of each raise you get will still be available to support additional spending.

All this plan does require is that when *new* money does come your way, you act on your plan to save a predetermined percentage of it right off the top. Simple, right? Doable? Absolutely! And you won't need to deny yourself anything you aren't already doing without, anyway.

So, if you are presently living paycheck to paycheck, think about how it might feel to have a growing margin of peace, as the total of your monthly expenses is slowly becoming less and less of what you earn. And think about how your financial peace of mind will be significantly enhanced.

This process is about as close as you can get to performing a sort of financial alchemy with your money. And, I believe, it is the single most powerful way for you to affirm the financial blessings you do receive.

When you do choose to take this single step, when you choose to follow The Plan to save one-half of every raise you receive from now on, you are giving powerful affirmation to your place in the future.

Chapter Sixteen

Gifts You Do Receive

*Repression of the life-force is the most common
reason I see people in therapy.*

—Thomas Moore, author of *Care of the Soul*

I believe that the failure to provide for your future is a
form of the repression that Thomas Moore is addressing in the
above quote. And, as I said, the knowledge that you are not
saving enough to adequately provide for the future is the reason
why many of us live with an undertow of dread in our lives.

Some of us can live with that dread better than others.
Some of us, after all, are better at fooling ourselves than others.
But ignoring the facts is not conducive to your well-being. This
subject reminds me of two relevant thoughts:

Things do not change, we change.

—Henry David Thoreau

And:

Wherever you go, there you are.

—Buddha

The one real way to deal with the dread of financial insecurity is to do something real about it.

Whatever amount you are able to reduce your present spending, using the exercises detailed in Step One, will be a good start. But the way that you will make your future different from your past is to do something different that will realize the desired change.

I would refer back to an earlier quote from Albert Einstein and make the point that what is required to change the results of thinking of one sort is thinking of another sort. If you have no plan to save and your present financial state is not a condition you want to persist, then you must do something different because, if you don't, it is almost a certainty that the same actions will lead to the same results.

I remember a conversation I had with a student once. She was thirty years old at the time and told me that she had $1,000 in savings. She told me that she had been working full-time since she was eighteen years old—over twelve years at the time of our discussion.

I asked her if she considered the amount she had saved sufficient and she told me she did not. I then told her that the chances were good that if she kept doing what she had been doing and thinking like she had been thinking over the past twelve years, by the time she was forty-two, she could expect to have $2,000 in savings.

I then asked her if she would be happy with that amount of savings at that age. When she told me that she would not be happy, I asked her what she planned to do differently to achieve a better result. Her answer was that she hoped to save more.

My point here is that hoping is not the action that is necessary to get where you want to be. Our actions are based, to a large extent, on our values. Our values reveal our thoughts. To achieve a different, more desirable result, think differently to act differently and establish goals that reflect different values.

The Fifty Percent Plan is the crux of that change. And, by taking the appropriate actions necessary to implement The Plan, you can't help but change your results for the better and make progress in the direction of your goals.

And, not only will you have a plan to save—the fundamental trait of most financially successful individuals—you will also become a good steward of the gifts that you do receive and someone who acknowledges your blessings in a real and powerful way.

Chapter Seventeen

How to Change You Luck

Concerning all acts of initiative and creation,
there is one elementary truth—that the moment
one definitively commits oneself, then
Providence moves too.

—Goethe

I believe there is no more powerful way to change your luck than to begin to live with a clearly defined purpose for your life, that is, to live an intentional life. And, as evidenced by the sentiments of the quote with which I open this chapter, I am not alone in believing that.

Your goals are what define your life's purpose and once you commit to a goal, suddenly fortune can move in your favor. Call it serendipity or call it luck, it is just the way the universe seems to work. If, on the other hand, you have no goals, you make it hard for luck to smile on you.

But a goal, in order to be an effective tool for personal or financial growth, must be measurable because if it isn't, then, you will not be able to measure your progress towards achieving that goal in any meaningful way. And, if you can't measure your progress, what good is a goal, at all?

But the reason why the goal to continually grow your margin is so effective is that it is so measurable. And, by breaking down that general overall goal into more specific intermediate goals, you can monitor your progress every step of the way.

The best time frame that I have found for those intermediate goals is one year. Then, simply by making a few assumptions about the rate at which your margin will grow, you will be able to project that growth into the future and to compare your actual results with those projections, year after year.

By setting an annual goal for the amount by which you want to grow your margin in the next twelve months, at the end of the year you will be able to determine whether or not you have met your goal and, if an adjustment is called for, exactly how much of an adjustment you will need to make.

And, again, the other half of every raise you receive is still yours to use at your discretion and as you see fit. If you choose to enhance some other aspect of your lifestyle, you can do so without any sense of guilt that you are doing so at the expense of your future.

However, if the value of increasing your savings is apparent to you, you might choose to dedicate the entire amount of the next few raises you receive to growing your margin. And, remember, the goal to save more is also the goal to spend less or, at least, to keep your expenses relatively fixed from now on.

The beauty of it is that you have the power to decide, now that you are aware that the option exists. Again, the secret is to identify, *in advance*, the money in your income and, then, to actually move it directly into your margin account.

By adhering to the Fifty Percent Plan I was eventually living on only one-half of my *gross* income and, as I have stated previously, saving about twenty-five percent. It took a while to get there but, when I did, it was a major boost to my level of financial peace of mind. And, later on in this book, I will share with you the options that will open up to you when you are saving that much of what you earn.

After a while, it occurred to me that I could project the growth of my margin simply by making a few basic assumptions. By doing so I was then able to measure my progress from year to year and tell whether or not I was on track to reach any particular goal. Being able to do that was very important to my ultimate success.

Remember—the most critical aspect of any goal you set is that you are able to measure your progress towards achieving it. Why is that so important? Because you can't manage what you can't measure!

It isn't rocket-science, or anything, but when I could actually see the numbers in black and white, it was just invigorating and motivating at the same time. If you do the same thing, that is, if you chart out the projected growth of your margin account, I think you will find it to be an invaluable exercise.

Not only will you find this to be a motivational tool, it is also the means by which you can monitor your progress and determine whether or not you are on track to reach your annual goal. If you reach a point in your timetable but you are not quite where you had projected, you can make adjustments or, perhaps, make cuts in your budget to make up the difference and get back on track.

The decision is yours but it is the act of having charted the projected growth of your margin that will provide you the feedback to know whether or not changes to your financial plan are necessary.

By the way, managing your progress in this way is a classic management tool commonly known as the *Plan-Do-Check-Act (PDCA) Cycle*. PDCA is a way to manage any project (and your goal to continually grow your margin is just that—a project) whereby you *plan* your actions, *do* (work) your plan, and, then, you periodically *check* your progress towards your goal.

If, at the check portion of the cycle, you are not where you need to be, you can then take the appropriate action (*act*) to correct your course. Once you have done so, the entire cycle simply repeats itself until the project is complete (or the goal achieved).

For example, assuming any base pay amount and an annual pay raise as a percentage of the base pay, you can project where you should be at any point in the future. In the following table are some sample projections that show how a margin of ten percent will grow based on a beginning income of $40,000 and assuming an annual pay raise equal to five percent:

Year	Income ($)	Margin ($)	%
1	40,000	4,000	10
2	42,000	5,000	11.9
3	44,100	6,050	13.7
4	46,305	7,153	15.4
5	48,620	8,311	17.1
6	51,051	9,588	18.8
7	53,604	10,804	20.3
8	56,284	12,211	21.7
9	59,099	13,618	23
10	62,054	15,095	24

As you can see, it will take about ten years to reach a twenty-five percent margin in that example. If, instead of only one-half of each raise, you saved the entire raise, you could reach your goal in half the time:

Year	Income ($)	Margin ($)	%
1	40,000	4,000	10
2	42,000	6,000	14
3	44,100	8,100	18
4	46,305	10,305	22
5	48,620	12,620	26

Following this example, you too can project and then track your progress in the growth of your margin on an annual basis. Unforeseen events that you can't anticipate when planning might help you grow your margin even faster than expected, as well.

For example, your raise might be more than the five percent assumed in the example, or you might get more than one raise in a single year.

It often seems to happen that we find ourselves becoming the beneficiaries of, what I can only describe as, fortuitous serendipity when we have a plan. The Roman philosopher I quoted earlier, Seneca, once said that no wind favors a ship without a destination. Whatever the opposite of that is, it is that force that is working in your favor when you are prepared to meet your good fortune with a plan already in place.

You now have a goal—to continually grow the percentage by which your income exceeds your costs of living. And, you also have a plan to get there that enables you to determine if you are on course to meet your projections every step of the way—The Fifty Percent Plan.

In the next step you learn how to further enhance your financial peace of mind by using your savings to bolster your financial well-being. The goal of Step Three is to build a financial safety net of savings equal to three to six months of living expenses.

Once this safety net is in place, you will be able to face the future and those proverbial (and inevitable!) slings and arrows of outrageous financial fortune with a higher level confidence and financial peace of mind.

Step Three, I call, *Hope For The Best...*

STEP THREE

Hope For The Best…

Chapter Eighteen

Here Comes That Rainy Day Feeling Again

So, if you have not been trustworthy in handling worldly wealth, who will trust you with true riches?

—Luke 16:11

Even when times are good, any reasonable adult will live with the faint tug of dread, anyway. It's a part of life because we all know that as quickly as life can take a turn for the better, it can, just as quickly, turn in the other direction.

Carl Jung, the man who has been called the father of modern psychotherapy, had the following words carved into the wood of his garden gate: *Summoned or not, the Gods will come.* I mean, if the father of modern psychotherapy was sweating the load like that, what chance do we have?

Any anxiety we experience associated with money, as real as it feels, however, is really the least of our worries. That thought, alone, should give you some relief when you find yourself in the middle of a sleepless night worrying about the bills…it should but it doesn't, I know.

The thing is, when the unexpected does happen, it almost always comes with a cost involved. Whether it is the car breaking down, a tooth that starts to ache, or the washing machine giving up the ghost, it is going to cost you.

Like I said, these are relatively minor annoyances in the grand scheme of things, but when you are living too close to the financial edge, what might otherwise be just another pain in the neck, could well prove to be that *last straw* that breaks your financial back.

The good news is that you can prepare yourself to meet most unexpected expenses with a little prior planning. The time to get an umbrella, however, is before it starts to rain. To do otherwise is to leave yourself exposed to whatever financial storms might blow in and, when the weather does turn on you, all the sudden you are scrambling for cover.

Being caught unprepared that way is, financially, a very dangerous situation to be in because under that sort of pressure a person can make some very bad decisions.

One common cause of the undertow of dread we live with is the knowledge that, despite our best intentions, plans do go awry. The best laid plans of mice and men…and *all* that. That dread, is the opposite of the financial peace of mind we all want to achieve and I am reminded of the lines from the John Lennon song, *Beautiful Boy*:

> *Before you cross the street,*
> *take my hand*
> *Life is what happens while you're busy*
> *making other plans*

Life *is* what happens while you're busy making other plans. But we need to make our plans, regardless, because while it is impossible to plan away every possible risk, financial risks are relatively easy to minimize almost to zero.

A financial rainy day is bound to dawn; you know that, I know that, we all know that. So why do so many of us get so wet when the day we knew was coming finally arrives? This is a book about getting *right* with money. You can't get right until you do right—until and unless you do the right *thing*. Until you do so, you will live with that subtle anxiety, that underlying dread, of knowing you *are* exposed.

The basic way you protect yourself, financially, in advance of the clouds gathering on the horizon, is simply to build your savings. There are other steps to take, but nothing will help you fend off the anxiety of the unknown like money in the bank. It is okay to hope for the best, we all do it, but it is just plain smart to plan for the worst.

Chapter Nineteen

Plan for the Worst

*Riches are not the end of life but an instrument
of life.*

—Henry Ward Beecher

Sure, you've heard this before and know it's important but until you actually have the money in the bank to cover three to six months of expenses readily available, you cannot understand the way it will enhance your financial peace of mind.

The savings you realize from reducing your expenses and growing your margin should be used, at first, exclusively to build a reserve of cash—what I call an Income Emergency Fund or *IEF*.

This account is not intended to meet predictable emergencies like those I mentioned earlier—the car, dentist, washing machine-kind of stuff. Those, although you can't predict exactly when they are likely to occur, or exactly how much they will wind up costing you, you do know they are coming and, so, you *can* plan for them. You will learn how to do that later in this book.

Your Income Emergency Fund is money standing by ready to meet the greatest financial threat most of us are likely to ever face—the loss of income. It is this threat of losing your income for an extended period that is the primary reason to have a financial safety net in place.

Usually, our income stream is interrupted when we lose our job for one reason or another—either we are laid-off, fired, or otherwise shown the door. The other thing that can happen to stop our paycheck is that we become physically incapable of working.

Now, some of us will be lucky enough to be covered by some form of income insurance, to one extent or another, in the event either of these financial storms blows in. But even if you are covered, delays in getting paid can make for some period of time when you are without income, nevertheless.

The other factor to consider is that neither type of insurance is likely to replace 100% of your previous income. That is another reason why it is so important that you not live on the financial edge of your earnings and also a reason to build a reserve even if you are counting on some other backup plan.

And, then, there are those of us who will have nothing to fall back on but our own initiative if the paychecks ever stop coming. In that case, your financial well-being is 100% dependent on you building a cash reserve, there in case your income ever stops coming in.

Now, you might be thinking that there is one other option I haven't mentioned—the remaining credit line on your charge cards. If that is what you are counting on to get you through should hard times descend, you should be aware of the downside of this strategy. While such a plan is better than no plan at all, it falls under the *any-port-in-a-storm* category.

You can't charge your rent or mortgage payment on a credit card. What you can do is get a cash advance, a very, very expensive cash advance, on a credit card or cards, as the case may be. But talk about robbing Peter to pay Paul! And the Peter we are referring to here is nothing less than your financial future.

If a financial storm does catch you unprepared, chances are your situation will go from bad to worse as you are forced to resort to debt, if that is even an option. The money to dig yourself out of the mess you're in is likely to be very expensive but you are forced to pay the price because you have no other choice.

The best way to avoid being swept under by a financial rip tide like that is simply to have a cushion of cash to see you through.

How much should you have in your Income Emergency Fund? That depends on several factors, including what it will take to let you sleep at night. All of us have our own unique comfort zone in this regard. I recommend you establish a goal to build your account to an amount equal to at least three months of living expenses, however, the ideal amount of your fund is closely tied to your personal employment situation.

If you are employed in an industry where it would be fairly easy to find a new job, three months worth of expenses is likely to prove adequate. On the other hand, if you know that finding a job in your field would probably take some time, you might need to build a fund equal to six months or more. You will be the best judge of this and, again, you need to factor in your own, personal comfort level.

If you're one of the lucky ones with unemployment and disability coverage, a three-month fund is likely to prove adequate. If you're not so lucky, a fund equal to six months of expenses will probably let you sleep a lot better at night. Ultimately, the exact amount is up to you; after all, you're the one who needs to sleep.

Chapter Twenty

More Gratitude, Expressed

*First, have a definite, clear, practical ideal—a
goal, an objective. Second, have the means to
achieve your ends—wisdom, money, materials,
and methods. Third, adjust all your means to
that end.*

—Aristotle

How does one go about building an Income Emergency
Fund? Well, obviously, you will need to take some amount of
your present day income and divert it to that end.

If you follow the suggestions in Steps One and Two, the
savings you realize by doing so will be the primary source of the
money to build your emergency fund. But in addition to those
steps, I also recommend that you plan to build this fund by
contributing at least one-half of every windfall or found money
that good fortune drops in your lap.

Like Step Two, having a plan in place and ready to act on to acknowledge your good fortune is a very self-affirming financial strategy. It will prevent these blessings from slipping through your fingers unaccounted for or that they simply disappear without a trace of the gift with which you were blessed.

So, every time some amount of *found* money does come your way, the first thing you do with half of it is tuck it away for a rainy day. That way, you will have tangible proof of your good fortune and it will have gone to a very good cause, indeed—your financial security.

How long it will take you to build your emergency fund to the desired amount depends on several factors, obviously. As a rule of thumb, however, if you are able to save ten percent of your monthly gross income it will take twenty-seven months to put aside an amount equal to three months of income and fifty-four months to build an amount equal to six months of income.

For example:

Monthly income:	$3,000	Total of
monthly Expenses:	$2,700	(90%)
Total of Three Month IEF:	$8,100	(3 x $2,700)
Amount Saved Monthly:	$300	(10%)
Months Required to Save $8,100:	27	($8,100/300)

Example Two:

Monthly income:	$3,000	
Total of Monthly Expenses:	$2,700	(90%)
Amount of Six Months Fund:	$16,200	(6 x $2,700)
Amount Saved Monthly:	$300	(10%)
Months Required to Save $16,200:	54	($16,200/300)

Now, you might be thinking that fifty-four or, even, twenty-seven months is a long time to leave yourself exposed to the financial weather but, remember, the day you begin to save is the day you at least have *something* set aside and also remember that it is growing.

And, by the way, my numbers don't include interest which, although not substantial at first, will add to the amount you are able to put away yourself.

Another point to consider here is that the figures in the previous table are based on saving ten percent of your income. The greater your margin, however, the faster your security will grow. And, if you see the obvious wisdom of having this account in place, you always have the option of reducing or eliminating one expense or another to speed up the process.

Any reductions in spending you make in order to grow your Income Emergency Fund can be viewed as temporary measures. Once your IEF is fully funded, you can then decide whether or not they belong back in your budget. And, remember, these are not really sacrifices, they are choices you make towards your goal of greater financial peace of mind.

Also keep in mind that it is unlikely that you will ever need to draw your emergency fund down to zero. With any luck at all, you will be able to restart your income stream before your IEF is completely exhausted. Your emergency fund is part umbrella and part security blanket to enhance the serenity with which you are able to face financial uncertainties. And, it will add tremendously to your sense of financial peace of mind even as it is growing.

Any extra amounts you are able to add to your emergency fund, be it found money or whatever, will go a long way towards getting it fully funded that much sooner. And also remember that the amount you are able to dedicate to building your fund will increase with every raise when you follow the plan outlined in Step Two.

Your IEF needs to be kept safe and close at hand. The best place to put the money in your fund is a money market account or a short-term certificate of deposit (CD). This is not money you want to put at risk in any way. It is not money you put in your favorite stock or loan to your brother-in-law for his latest get-rich-quick scheme. This is your sleep-tight money.

As the amount of your fund grows, you might consider what is known as a "CD Ladder." A CD Ladder is built by staggering the maturity date of each CD one month apart, each CD for an amount equal to whatever amount it will take to cover one month of expenses. A CD Ladder allows you to commit to a longer deposit term on some of your money and, so, you can probably get a slightly better interest rate. But, hey, a little more is better than a little less and every little bit helps!

If you are not certain of the details involved in building a CD Ladder, simply ask about it at whatever bank or financial institution your IEF is deposited. Or you can search the term on the internet for all the information you'll ever need on the subject.

An Income Emergency Fund will not prevent financial emergencies but it will make their prospect much less daunting. And, until that rainy day does arrive, you *can* sleep tight knowing you've got it covered.

Chapter Twenty-One

Rainy Day Redux

Money can't buy me love.

—The Beatles

The question this issue of having an Income Emergency Fund raises, however, is this: What can you do to protect yourself until your account builds to some meaningful amount? Fortunately, you have a few options to minimize your exposure until then.

One option is, of course, to take more drastic measures to grow your fund faster. If the thought of being without a financial safety net really bothers you, and you have already cut your budget to the bone, this is one situation where the extra income from a part-time job would prove really beneficial.

If you dedicate one-hundred percent of the income from that job to building your IEF, it should add up pretty quick. Another step you can take is to get proactive about planning a fallback position in the event of a loss of income. That would mean having a plan in place that you could then call on if the worst did happen.

A plan to do so would include a list of your present expenses identified as the first to go in case of a financial emergency. Just having this plan in place, and knowing exactly how *little* you could live on in case of a financial emergency, should help you feel a little better, at least.

And, then, there *is* that (pseudo) liquidity in the form of the available credit line on your credit cards, as was covered earlier. A better option, if you are a homeowner with some equity in your property, is a home-equity line of credit. But don't wait until you are unemployed to apply for one because your chances of being approved will not be as good. What you need to do is apply for it *before* you need it and while you still have an income.

But credit is just never as good an option as cash simply because debt will always have to be paid back. If you rely on a loan or some other form of credit for income during a financial emergency, when you do restart your income you will have payments on that new debt that you didn't have before. So, although debt is not the best answer, you do need to include a credit contingency in your planning until your IEF is in place.

Now, I know that three to six months of income is likely to represent a sizable amount of money for many of you reading this. And, I know, that there are all sorts of schemes out there to cover your assets in some other way.

Some well-intentioned financial advisors will tell you that the interest rate you realize on money in the bank argues against keeping it *that* liquid. But this is not a book of typical financial strategies. This *is* a book about taking steps towards greater financial peace of mind.

So, repeat after me: money in the stock market cannot be counted on to be there when you need it. Money *bet* on Wall Street is a fair-weather friend. Peace of mind does not flow from the *chance* of a couple of extra percentage points in interest. If you want a higher net worth *and* greater financial peace of mind, the answer is not to take more risk—the answer is to save more!

Chapter Twenty-Two

Double Jeopardy

*We can all have our own opinions but we can't
all have our own facts.*

—Senator Patrick Moynihan

An Income Emergency Fund is simply a common sense tool to maintain a necessary level of financial viability we all should have. It is just too dangerous to be without a certain amount of cash liquidity, also known as money in the bank.

But as important as it is to have your fund in place, there is a financial jeopardy *out there* that is even greater than the threat of unemployment. The number one cause of personal bankruptcies cited in court records across the country, by far, is medical bills.

Most people, because of the press the subject receives, would probably guess that credit card debt is the major reason that people declare bankruptcy. In fact, credit card debt is seldom the reason why people go broke.

If you are mired in credit card debt, that could be perceived as good news, if little consolation. But the fact is that most of us are OK with handling our credit cards. And recovery from even large amounts of this kind of debt is possible without having to resort to the poison pill of bankruptcy.

The reason that medical bills represent such a financial risk is that they can simply overwhelm even a sizable Income Emergency Fund in fairly short order. That is, unless, you do some sound planning to suitably address the issue.

The only real protection from this very real threat is the right kind of medical insurance. Now, this is not a book about insurance planning but it is an issue that must be addressed as part of achieving financial peace of mind.

The whole issue of medical insurance in this country is terribly convoluted (don't get me started!). But if you don't have it, for whatever reason, you are, absolutely, taking a huge risk.

And, because it is so risky, it should be the first issue you address as you follow the steps and begin to make some room in your budget—even before you begin funding your Income Emergency Fund, you should use your savings to purchase a minimum level of medical insurance.

One policy, in particular, to consider is what is known as "catastrophic coverage." This is a policy that will cover all medical expenses over a fixed amount known as the plan deductible. The exact dollar-size of the deductible that is right for you depends on several financial factors so, please, talk to an expert to determine what will best suit your particular needs.

To choose the medical insurance coverage that is right for you, you will absolutely need more information than what I have just provided; all I want to do here is to stress just how important medical insurance is to your peace of mind.

Even if you have medical insurance, however, you are not, absolutely, out of the woods on this issue. Surprisingly, many of those who go bankrupt due to medical bills have medical insurance; it was the gaps in their coverage that caused problems.

My policy caps my annual out of pocket expenses at $5,000. That means that the most I will have to pay for covered charges is that amount and, then, insurance pays the rest. That is the similar to the provision in the catastrophic-type policy I mentioned before. Again, talk to a reputable insurance agent and shop around in order to evaluate the various options.

I budget for a certain amount of uninsured medical expenses every year, such as co-pays and other deductibles. Any amount left in this account at the end of the year, I then roll over into my IEF. The only reason I would ever dip into that fund other than unemployment would be to pay medical expenses after the balance in that medical account had been depleted.

In this chapter, I raised the issue of debt but in the next chapter I will address it in more depth. Step Four towards greater financial peace of mind is to *Pay the Minimum*.

STEP FOUR

Pay the Minimum

Chapter Twenty-Three

The Three Faces of Spending

I am indeed rich, since my income is superior to my expense, and my expense is equal to my wishes.

—Edward Gibbon

Money you earn today is spent on either yesterday, today, or tomorrow. Few of us ever take the time to think about their income as divided up like that but we should because there are some powerful implications to that statement.

You get your check and some of it is spent in the present to pay for today's expenses. That much is fairly obvious. The rent, light bill, and gas for your car are all examples of money spent in the present on present-day costs of living.

That portion of your income that you put away for the future is put there in anticipation of spending that will take place at some later date. Money you set aside in a retirement account, for example, is put there to fund the spending you will do after you leave the workforce.

Then, there is the money that is taken from today's income to pay for yesterday's spending. This is the money that goes to pay your debts. Debt from past consumption can be like a ghost that haunts you in the here and now. Other than unemployment, perhaps nothing is less conducive to financial peace of mind than debt.

First let's get clear on what I'm talking about here. Expenditures can be grouped into one of two categories: *debt* or *expense*. An *expense* can be thought of as a cost of living that will never go away. For example, utility bills, gas for your car, or groceries are each an expense.

A *debt*, on the other hand, is a bill that can be paid off and, when paid off, it goes away. A car loan is one example of a debt and medical bills are another. But the debt that too many of us are most familiar with is credit card bills.

Expenses are a fact of life but debt is not; that is a very important distinction that you need to keep reminding yourself of because nothing will enhance your financial peace of mind in quite the same way as will being debt-free. Even though most of us accept debt as if it is an inevitable part of our financial life—it is not! But in our society, getting to debt-free will definitely be a swim against the mainstream.

Now, I know, certain kinds of debt are not necessarily all bad. Going into debt in anticipation of a larger, future benefit can be thought of as something of an investment; student loans are often considered in this light. But all debt does diminish our present-day resources and, in that sense, has a negative element to it.

The money we spend making payments on our debt is money we cannot otherwise allocate either to the present or the future. So, our debt costs us the opportunity to spend our money more wisely or in some way that we would prefer.

The more present-day income that is used to pay for yesterday's spending the more opportunity we lose. So, it should be fairly obvious to you that the less of our present-day income that goes to pay our debts, the better. Ideally, we would live without that debt element to our spending but, instead, debt is a real problem for many of us.

Of particular concern for far too many of us is debt that is of no present day value, that is, that does not reflect positively on the bottom line of your net worth statement; that kind of debt is, basically, *worthless*. Most debt of this sort was usually charged to one credit card or another and went to support spending that was beyond the capacity of our income.

Once we begin to use credit cards to finance spending our present income cannot support, we can find ourselves locked into a sort of self-perpetuating cycle. And, if we allow ourselves to become accustomed to this artificial level of spending, we will find the amount of our debt steadily growing. This scenario is actually a kind of trap that more and more of us are falling into every day.

You see, if you allow the total of your credit card debt to grow, then the monthly total of even the minimum payment (or payments, if you owe on more than a single card) will also grow. What this means is that your income is effectively going down and, so, you will need to take on even more debt to pick up the slack. When you find yourself in this situation it can seem like there is no way to escape as your debt continues to grow as if it had a life of its own.

As bad as that situation is, however, the larger issue is the effect that worthless debt can have on your ability to fund the other two elements of spending—today and tomorrow. In particular, it is our future that is almost certain to suffer because, when your income is going down, the least painful of the three pots to dip into is the one labeled "*tomorrow*."

Unfortunately, what many people do who find themselves trapped in this cycle of growing debt is to compound the mistake by taking a reflexive but unconsidered approach to address the problem. They spend too much, too soon, in attempt to pay down their debt leaving nothing to invest in tomorrow. When they do that it is yet another example of robbing Peter to pay Paul.

It is difficult to predict *precisely* how much money we will need in the future to fund our future financial independence but most of us just *know* when we're not saving enough. And you definitely know you will come up short if you are not saving anything at all!

One way to judge your financial position is to think about it in terms of what percentage of your income is going towards each of the three elements of spending—past, present, and future. If more than ten percent of your income is being spent on debt other than your mortgage, you could have a problem.

In fact, when the percentage of your income going to debt payments is above the eight percent range, mortgage lenders will begin to reduce the amount they are willing to loan you. That is an indication of what lenders think about spending on the past. They realize that, not only is it indicative of a problem today, they know it can be a strong indication of more problems yet to come.

And eight percent, if you think about, will not finance much in the way of debt. If you are earning $40,000 a year, eight percent of that is only about $250 a month. That is less than the amount of most new car loans.

Now, if, on the other hand, you stop and consider what it would mean to have a continually growing margin of peace, that is, that the amount you are managing to save is continually growing, the picture changes entirely. It will mean that the percentage of your income available to fund future spending is steadily increasing and, with it, your financial peace of mind.

Getting rid of worthless debt *will* help to accelerate the growth in your margin but there are other, more important, financial considerations to be weighed before you go rushing headlong into that breach.

Chapter Twenty-Four

Do the Right Thing

A penny saved is a penny earned.

—Ben Franklin

First, let me further define worthless debt for you. Debt is either secured or unsecured. A mortgage, for example, is *secured* by property. If you don't pay your mortgage, you lose your house. A car loan is also a secured loan.

Another aspect of a secured debt is that the object underlying that debt will usually retain some part or all of its initial value. New cars depreciate rapidly at first but, then, more gradually. Real estate will usually hold its value and, in fact, will often appreciate. And, even though the debt owed will be listed on the liability side of your net worth statement, the present-day market value of that object will also reflect positively on the assets side of the equation.

Unsecured debt is both unsecured and the value of the debt is almost entirely *consumed* at purchase—that's why I refer to worthless debt as *consumer* debt. A good example of consumer debt is a restaurant meal paid for on a credit card. You are left with the debt but nothing to show for it. But, if you don't pay the bill when it comes due, it is not as if they can come to your house and take the meal back!

So, the only place unsecured consumer debt usually shows up is on the liability side of the ledger without any positive entry to offset it on the assets side—it is, in fact, worse than worthless because it is dragging down the total of your net worth.

As an exercise, figure out exactly how much you are spending every month on debt repayment excluding your mortgage payment, if you have one. If you are like most people, that number might be as high as twenty percent of your gross income, or more, especially if you are have a car loan. If you were to add in your mortgage, assuming you have one, that figure might just climb to fifty percent or more!

Are lenders crazy or something? I mean, how can they let people get in debt to the tune of fifty percent of their income and expect them to keep paying the bills? In fact, it used to be that lenders were *extremely* wary of unsecured debt and understandably so. After all, a person could just walk away from such debt and leave the lender, *holding the bag,* so to speak. It was this *unsecured* aspect of some lending that had to be addressed before the credit industry could become the financial juggernaut it is today.

The stroke of genius that made *easy credit* for unsecured debt a reality was the invention of the individual credit history. It made it much more consequential for a borrower to simply walk away from their debt with impunity because if you did so, your ability to borrow in the future, for any debt whatsoever, secured or not, was severely impaired.

If you wreck your credit these days because you can't keep up with debt you owe on credit cards, it is likely to keep you from ever getting a home mortgage. And, too, many employers are now checking the credit history of job applicants to ferret out potential problems.

Individual credit histories were an absolute stroke of genius for the financial industry but not such a boon to individual consumers. Now, you can't just ignore a creditor's call because they can take something from you of real value— your credit rating!

Most unsecured consumer debt is owed on credit cards of one sort or another although unsecured spending is sometimes financed with what is known as a *signature* loan. If you qualify, all you need to do to get a signature loan is sign the loan documents. You do not need any other form of collateral to secure the loan other than your signature and that is why it is called a signature loan. Signature loans, like credit cards, are a form of unsecured debt.

When someone is trapped in the cycle of growing consumer debt, the situation can feel hopeless but it is not hopeless. You have the power to turn it around and just being aware that you have that power should give you *some* hope. But it is a power that must be used correctly if you are to achieve the desired results.

When you find yourself in a situation that is causing you a problem, the first step to recovery is to face the facts and accept them for what they are. The next step is to formulate a plan to change the situation and begin to move in the desired direction.

Sometimes, though, people panic and do not sufficiently think out their response. When it comes to repaying debt, consumer credit card debt in particular, the initial reaction is usually the desire to want to pay it off as soon as possible. When you react that way, however, you give up the power you have to take control of your financial situation in a more positive way.

Chapter Twenty-Five

Good Intentions Gone Bad

First secure an independent income, then
practice good virtue.

—Greek saying

Most of us understand that consumer debt is not a good *thing*. Those of us living with a level of debt that we find troubling usually feel the urge to eliminate it as soon as possible. Unfortunately, rushing to pay off your debts will often serve to only make the situation worse.

Almost always, when someone is faced with an aggravating amount of consumer debt they attack the debt as if that was the problem—it is not! Debt is only the symptom of the actual problem. The real problem is what caused you to go in debt in the first place—your spending!

First, let's look at what happens when someone attacks the symptom rather than the problem. The likely scenario will go something like this: It is that time of the month when you sit down to pay the bills. Usually, this occurs right after you have received your latest paycheck so you're feeling a bit flush. Your bills are laid out before you and those three or four (or more!) credit card bills irk you to no end.

You have heard all the horror stories of how long it will take and how much it will cost in interest if you make only the minimum payment due, so, in an effort to avoid that fate, you decide to send in a little *extra*.

But, when you are living paycheck to paycheck and particularly if you are spending more than you earn, it is almost always the case that even that little extra is too much and more than you can actually afford. So, when you do pay more than you can afford, what will usually happen then is you will run out of money before your next check arrives.

There is no such thing as *extra* money. Certainly, there was not any in your paycheck, so where did that extra you paid at the front-end come from? It can only come off the back-end, of course. That extra you paid at the beginning of the month will leave you short at the end of the month and needing to cover the shortfall, again. What else can you do, since you have nothing left from your paycheck, except resort to charging that shortfall on a credit card?

Instead of making any progress, when you pay more than you can afford, all you will have accomplished is made it almost certain that you will, once again, come up short at the end of the month. In other words, you have accomplished nothing!

When someone attempts to pay off their debt faster than they can afford to do so, a bad outcome is not only possible but likely. Our debts are the result of poor spending choices we made in the past but you can't do anything to change the past. But what you can do is change how you spend from now on, in the present, one day at a time.

Your focus, then, should be not on your debts but on your daily spending because it is the only place you can exercise any true measure of control. That is not to say that you will not take steps intended to get out of debt, you will, but those steps will not be the focus of your efforts.

It was your spending that created the debt in your life. As I explained, debt comes from living beyond your means and spending more than you earn. The first step is to do what is necessary to stop the situation from getting worse and that step is to choose to spend differently to achieve a different outcome.

Chapter Twenty-Six

Zen and the Art of Debt-Free Living

*If you would seek peace, stop chasing so many
things.*

—Buddha

The first step to a more reasonable approach to settling your debts is to accept the fact that it will take about as long to get out of debt as it took you to get into it. After all, the chains of debt in which you now find yourself were cast one link at a time. And it is in that same way that the problem is best resolved.

If you are $5,000 in debt and it took you three years to get there, it will take you about three years to get out: Accept that and move on for it is the way to debt-free and prosperous living.

You will not get out of debt overnight but you can, over time. Do not try to rush the process. That mentality is just a reflection of the desire for *instant gratification* that got you into this mess in the first place. Don't let your debts exert any more power in your life than is already the case; calm down, remain calm and get a little Zen about it.

More and more, people are resorting to home equity lines of credit to pay off consumer debts. I think this trend will lead to more foreclosures than ever because it only addresses the symptom not the problem. In fact, people are using these loans to enable even higher levels of consumer debt beyond the carrying capacity of their incomes.

The same dynamic is at work when someone gets relief from their debts through bankruptcy. They have done nothing to address the problem that led to their debt.

Home equity lines of credit and bankruptcy are financial tools that do have their place, but when used to alleviate the ills of overspending, they are not the most prudent course. In fact, they are often mistakes, themselves.

It will help you to come to terms with your consumer debt if you accept your debts as simply the symptom of the actual issue which is spending. Do not fall into the trap of giving up the power you have to settle your debts in a way that is most conducive to your own well being. That power can be summed up in three simple words: Pay the minimum!

I know it sounds counter-intuitive somehow and, certainly, it goes against the more popular wisdom of the day but, the fact is, there are better ways to spend your money than repaying consumer debt. Certainly, it will need to be repaid, but that repayment should be made on a schedule that is most conducive to your financial well-being.

The reason you are reading this book is to learn steps that will increase your financial peace of mind. You won't make any real progress towards that goal by attacking a symptom of what is actually causing your debt. And, when you do pay the minimum, you will not only take control over your debts, you will be able to forget them, altogether!

Paying off your debts is not and should not be allowed to become your most important financial goal. There are many goals that should come before it. The dreams your goals represent and your future, for example.

Certain steps take precedence over other steps in achieving greater financial peace of mind. That is important to remember because, the fact is, our financial resources are not unlimited. Settling your debts is less important than Step Three, establishing an Income Emergency Fund, for example. But it is possible to achieve positive outcomes on two fronts at the same time.

Remember, money you earn in the present goes either to support spending you have done in the past, the expenses you have today, or spending you plan to do in the future. In other words, our money has a lot of work to do. By paying the minimum, you will be addressing the issue of yesterday *but* with the least amount of negative impact on more important priorities.

In this way, you focus on what is truly important, your future, but without losing sight of concerns that still need to be addressed. On the other hand, and in comparison, when you choose to pay more than the minimum on your debts, what you are telling yourself, in a very real sense, is that your debts are *more* important than both your dreams and your future.

Are they? Of course not! You only have so much money after all. So, what's it going to be—your debts or your dreams? But before you jump to any conclusions here, let me explain the plan in more detail.

My Pay-the-Minimum Plan actually has two phases to it. Phase One applies until you have that six-months worth of expenses stashed in savings. Once you have that amount saved, you then transition to Pay-the-Minimum Phase Two.

The amount you pay during Phase One will be the actual total of the minimums required on all your variable credit card debt. For example, if you have three credit cards and the total of the minimum payments due is $100, then that is how much you will pay that month—$100.

Next month, assuming no new charges, the total of the minimum payments due will be slightly lower. And, assuming the total of all your other expenses has remained the same, you will have more money to put away in savings. Not much, I know, but when your financial security is shaky, every little bit helps. And, not only that, the total of your monthly expenses will also be that much lower.

Again, not much lower, I know, but, combined with other reductions you are able to make, your financial position is better than it was last month. And it will better still next month and the month after that and, if you stick to The Plan, from now on!

Once you have achieved your savings goal of having an amount equal to six months worth of living expenses in the bank, it is time to move into Phase Two of the Pay-the-Minimum Plan.

In Phase Two the strategy changes a little. Whereas in Phase One you were paying less and less each month, now that you have achieved your savings goal your financial position is such that you afford to apply more towards paying off your debts—but not much more—because your money still has a lot of work to do!

In Phase Two you take whatever the total of all the "minimum" payments required is equal to in the first month after you have achieved your savings goal and freeze that as the monthly amount you will pay towards your debts, from that point forward, until they are completely paid off.

Let's say, for the sake of example, that you owe $5,000 in total consumer debt. It really doesn't matter to the process whether you owe this amount on one credit card or one dozen. What does matter, and the number you will need to know in order to implement Phase Two, is the total amount of all the minimum payments due at this point in time.

The card companies generally require a minimum payment of about four percent of the outstanding balance owed on the card. In this example, then, that would amount to $200. We will label the month in which you sent in that $200 payment as Phase Two/Month One.

If you were to pay that amount and not incur any new charges, the next month the minimum payment *required* would be slightly less than $200. But what you do is continue to send in the same amount as you did in Month One, a total of $200.

Now this next step in the process is very important:

When you pay one bill off, you take the money you were paying on that bill and add it to the payment amount of whichever remaining bill has the highest interest rate. When that bill is paid in full, you move on to the next using the same strategy until all your consumer debts are paid in full.

(By the way, back in 2005, Congress passed a law requiring the credit cards companies to raise their minimum payment requirement from two percent to four percent of the amount owed. They did this to protect consumers. Likewise, the monthly amount you pay in Phase Two should be no less than that same four percent of the balance due. If you have a card that is still requiring that two percent amount, figure out what the four percent amount comes to and that will be the amount you lock in as the amount you will pay in Phase Two.)

Once the plan is in place, you can then forget about these bills because they will eventually be paid off—but only if you stop adding to the total of your credit card debt. And, what that means, of course, is that you must stop spending (and charging!) more than you earn. Breaking the credit card habit is the only way you will ever settle your debts.

The plan to pay-the-minimum has a better chance of succeeding than does paying some larger amount for one very good reason—it leaves you more income. And the more income you keep, the less likely you are to come up short at the end of the month.

At first this might not be much but—hey!—twenty bucks less to a credit card bill means twenty bucks more in your pocket and that much less of a chance that you will be forced to incur new credit card debt to make up the difference!

Remember, the first two goals of The Plan are, one, to help you bring your spending into alignment with what you earn, and, two, to help you build your savings. But the third goal of The Plan is that you not only pay off your debts but that you do so in a way that is most likely to help you achieve goals number one and two, as well.

And, as previously mentioned, once you have reached Phase Two, you can, pretty much, forget about your credit card debts, entirely, and start thinking about ways to grow your savings. Can you see how the plan to pay-the-minimum changes your life?

Now when you think about your finances, the eight-hundred pound gorilla in the room is all that money you owe—you are focused on the negative. Once you put your plan in action, however, you can begin to think about how your financial situation is improving and how you have taken control of the situation. You have gone from powerless to empowered!

Can you see the difference in the two mindsets? And, when you shift the focus in this way, you will have taken an enormous and enormously liberating stride towards greater financial peace of mind!

Chapter Twenty-Seven

A Change of Focus

In the last analysis, our only freedom is the
freedom to discipline ourselves.

—Bernard Baruch

Once you have implemented my Pay-The-Minimum Plan, it is time to turn your efforts to addressing what it was caused you to go into debt in the first place—overspending.

Remember, the first definition of overspending is spending more in any one month than you earned in that month. Spending is best managed on a month to month basis because it is provides a timeframe to your budgeting that most of us can most readily relate to.

The goal, then, is to reduce your spending on that same monthly basis and to not incur any new debt. As simple as that might sound, however, it can prove difficult to rein in your spending once you are trapped in that cycle of overspending and growing debt.

Again, the trick is to comb your present day expenses and expenditures with an eye towards reducing where you can to create some immediate space in your budget. It is that space that will allow you to put your credit cards away.

Any reductions you can make in your budget will help, of course, but you should aim to reduce your monthly spending by a percentage equal to the total of your consumer debt divided by your total annual income.

For example, let's say you owe a total of $4,000 in consumer debt and that your annual income is $40,000. $4,000 divided by $40,000 equals ten percent (4,000/40,000 = 0.1) and that would be the *target* amount by which you would aim to cut your monthly spending. Why? Because that percentage figure is likely to be *approximately* the same amount by which, on average, you are overspending every month.

Your actual figure might be higher or lower than that in the example but, in order to reduce your monthly budget at all, you will need to have a monthly budget in the first place.

Depending on your particular situation, severe measures might even be required but, as severe as they might appear, you should remember that any inconvenience or discomfort they might cause you are likely to be short-lived. These are steps taken to right your ship and they do not necessarily have to represent long-term lifestyle adjustments.

You see, even if the amount by which you are overspending from month to month is not a lot, the months add up quickly and small amounts can add up to a substantial sum almost before you realize what is happening. Then, even if do manage to keep the wolves at bay, your growing debt will become the cause of more and more stress.

So, how do we respond to the stress of all these bills piling up? Well, if you listen to the pundits and what passes for good advice these days, you send in *extra* money you really don't have just to feel as if you are doing something about the problem. But there is no such thing as *extra* money—all your money has a job to do!

And, when you do send in that extra (not really extra!) money, what will usually happen next is that the last paycheck will run out before the next paycheck comes in. And it is in that gap where we are *forced* to resort to credit. What you need to do is close that gap by paying the minimum and cutting expenses.

It *is* possible to step off the debt treadmill and the way to do that is by finding whatever room you can in your present spending to give yourself some breathing room. Hold a garage sale, stop eating at restaurants, join a carpool, turn off cable TV service; drastic times call for drastic measures but, remember, it is not forever it is, at worst, a temporary inconvenience.

And, really, in the grander scheme of things, it's your financial security and peace of mind that are at stake. The measures mentioned, after all, represent a choice you make to achieve a more positive outcome not a sacrifice.

A sacrifice is when parents choose to go without eating so that their children will have enough. It is not a sacrifice when you choose to forego dinner out and keep those thirty or forty dollars in your pocket and off your credit card balance.

Later on, when your financial position is stronger, it is likely that you will have the money to add some of the cuts you made back into your budget, if you choose to do so. But the chances are that, after you have lived without something for awhile, you might just decide you didn't need it, after all!

In an earlier chapter I covered the process of combing through your expenditures to look for spending to cut from your budget. This is an absolutely critical exercise and what you want to accomplish, through the process of closely examining your spending, is to make it less likely that you will need to resort to debt to prop up your spending.

It is generally accepted that there are two types of spending, *discretionary* and *non-discretionary*. Those expenses or debt payments that we are absolutely obligated to pay represent non-discretionary spending. This includes expenditures such as court-mandated payments, child-support payments, for example.

Some people put expenditures such as rent, the mortgage payment, and utilities in the non-discretionary category but I do not think they *absolutely* belong there. Some part of the spending we do on food can, certainly, be defined as non-discretionary. I mean, we all need to eat. But at least some of the food most of us buy we could just as easily do without and, so, it actually represents discretionary spending.

Discretionary spending is just that—spending subject to your discretion. And, whether it's a variable expense like groceries or gas for your car, or a debt with the same fixed amount due every month like your mortgage or a car payment, what you want to do is reduce or eliminate some of your discretionary spending in order to create a margin between what you earn and what you spend.

Let me give you a tip—all of your spending is discretionary. Accepting that statement as a fact is the first step to changing the belief system that has led to many of our money problems. Even court-mandated payments are subject to review if your financial situation is dire enough to truly (*truly*) warrant it.

Rent, food, utilities, car payments, even the mortgage are all subject to being considered for being cut to create some immediate space between what you earn and what you spend. And, depending on just how deep you're willing to cut, changing the course of your financial life might well result in taking some drastic measures.

These measures could include selling your house and moving into a rental, finding a roommate to share living expenses, selling a car on which you have a loan and using the proceeds to buy a car for which you can pay cash—heck, it might mean selling the car and taking the bus for awhile.

The extent to which you are willing to go depends entirely on how much you value your financial peace of mind. The process includes facing up to accepting the life you can actually afford to live based on your income. This does not mean you will be locked into this life forever. Your income will increase and as you settle your debts you will free up more money to fund lifestyle enhancements.

But, remember, it is very likely that many of the material goods on which you are presently spending your money are like beads for Manhattan—they are robbing you of your potential not enhancing the likelihood of your achieving it!

No, not every dollar you spend will find its way to your bottom line but that should at least be a consideration in the transaction because it is that consideration that will help you measure the *true* cost of every purchase you make.

And, when I say true cost, I mean the cost in terms of the negative effect your spending is having on your peace of mind, financial and otherwise. Peace of mind is a zero-sum equation; all aspects of your life add *or* subtract from your bottom line in that regard. If your worries are keeping you awake at night it doesn't matter what the exact cause of those worries are, you are awake, nevertheless.

The shovel that most people use to dig their financial hole is credit cards. If that applies to you, let me say this, again—you can't make any real progress until you break the charge card habit. That is the fundamental rule of eliminating debt from your life.

To do that, to break your dependence on credit to artificially supplement your income, you need to make the commitment that you will spend what you earn but absolutely no more as you begin the process of living the Seven Steps.

Once you are clear on that, you then begin the process of being really conscious of every dollar you spend. This is an on-going process of examining every item in your budget and every entry in your spending diary with an eye towards reducing, deferring, or eliminating wherever and whenever possible in order to grow your margin of peace.

A big step in controlling your spending will be to leave your credit cards at home and to spend using only cash—not checks, not debit cards—cash! The main reason to pay with cash is because various surveys have revealed that we tend to spend somewhere between ten and thirty percent *more* when we shop with a credit card.

At some intuitive level, you can probably understand this phenomenon. When you pay with plastic, it doesn't quite feel as real as when you count out your hard-earned dollars. But, remember, the foundation of greater financial peace of mind is to spend with a *greater* awareness of each transaction.

When you spend using a credit card, or even a check or debit card, you are taking just the opposite approach—you are *distancing* yourself from the transaction and it is that distance that makes it much easier to spend more than you had planned to and, even, more than you have.

I mean, after all, credit cards and debit cards and checking accounts were all invented to make it easier for you to spend. Spending should not be easier.

Yes, if you are going to pay with cash, you will need to plan your shopping more carefully—but that is a good thing! Yes, you will need to leave the house with enough cash to cover what you plan to buy but, again, that will keep you from spending more than you had planned to spend. And, if you only have enough cash for those items on your shopping list, you won't have enough for any impulsive buying.

No one needs more than one or, at the most, two credit cards. If you have more than that, now is the time to consider closing some of those accounts as it is in no way helpful to carry a bunch of credit cards around with you when you shop.

If you are presently counting on the credit limit on those extra cards to fall back on in case of a financial emergency, you should at least leave them at home. Or, better yet, keep them secured in a safety deposit box; that way they will not be so readily available. Then, as the growing balance in your margin account permits, you can close those accounts.

(And one more note here: Just cutting up the card will not close the account. To close the account you need to actually call or write the company and direct them to do so.)

Chapter Twenty-Eight

Driven To Extremes

Virtue is in the mean, not the extreme.

—Aristotle

There is a repayment hierarchy into which your consumer debts can be placed. The higher the interest rate you are paying on any individual debt, the higher in the repayment hierarchy it *should* be ranked.

Another factor to consider in ranking a debt for payoff is the effect it has on the bottom line of your net worth. Unsecured consumer debt, for example, will almost always drag your net worth down. This is because the debt is entered on the liability side of your net worth statement but there is no entry to offset it, even partially, on the asset side of the ledger. Paying off this kind of debt should be a priority.

If you are already free of consumer debt you are in a great financial position but the effect of some secured debts on your net worth can be just as negative; vehicles are a prime example of this. Let's now explore this issue in more depth as it is an important concept:

For many of us, the equity in our homes represents a large portion of our net worth. And this makes sense because, for most of us, our home is almost always the largest single purchase we will ever make.

If you are buying your home, the outstanding balance of the mortgage on it represents a liability but its market value represents an asset entry on the positive side of your net worth statement. Vehicles on which we carry a loan will also impact both sides of our net worth statement in that same way.

When you purchase a vehicle, a new vehicle in particular, the net affect on your net worth can, sometimes, be negative. That condition is referred to as being *upside down* in that loan and it is a result of owing more on the vehicle than it would be likely to sell for.

You have probably heard the term, "house-rich but cash-poor." It is usually used to refer to someone whose house payment leaves them with little slack in their budget and is meant to imply that someone has over-extended in order to finance their home.

It is my experience, however, that more people today are *car-rich but cash-poor* than ever before, having committed to financing vehicles that are draining their resources away from funding more important financial needs. And a person will voluntarily put his or herself into this position and gladly take the financial hit just to be able to drive a vehicle they really can't afford and could just as easily do without!

House-rich and car-rich might seem to be the same sort of financial condition but only until you take a look at the impact that each has on your bottom line. A $25,000 car will lose something like twenty percent of its value the minute you drive it off the dealer's lot. That amounts to an instant loss of $5,000 that gets subtracted right off the bottom line of your net worth statement.

And the impact on your net worth will usually get even worse from that point! If you have a five-year loan on a vehicle, it is likely that the negative impact to your net worth at the end of year one will be as high as thirty percent or more of the original purchase price. And all the payments you have been making are no where to be seen—they have only served to limit the total of the negative impact!

It is a very different picture when you look at the affect that being house-poor will have on your net worth. If your home has a present-day value of $200,000 and is appreciating five percent a year, that $10,000 in appreciation in the coming year will *add* to and grow your net worth. And—check this out—the amount of that appreciation is compounded one year to the next if the market continues to rise! Compounded appreciation is the only financial force more powerful than compounded interest!

Also, the payments you make serve to pay down the principal amount of the mortgage and add even more to the total of your assets. So, as you can see, there is a very big difference between being house-poor and being car-poor.

Meanwhile, the auto industry is doing all they can to make it as easy as possible for you to fall into their trap. The auto industry offers all sorts of smoke and mirror financing and sales incentives to move their products; giving with one hand while taking away with the other. It's the oldest con in the world!

Zero-interest loans are just one version of this slight of hand. Those who fall victim to zero-interest financing often pay top-dollar for their vehicle, losing any benefit of the seemingly favorable financing terms.

When you factor in all the other costs of driving and the fact that most families own two vehicles or more, transportation costs can literally go through the roof and end up costing you much more than what you pay for your home over a lifetime of buying and driving vehicles.

The Automobile Association of America estimated that the average total cost to operate a private vehicle in 2003 was fifty-six cents per mile. This includes vehicle acquisition costs and operating costs such as fuel and insurance.

If you drive just 15,000 miles a year and drive for 50 years, the two car total comes to 1,500,000 miles and at a cost of $840,000! If you could you cut that figure in half, you could add as much as $500,000 to your net worth by the time you retire.

Now, if you are in your twenties or thirties, retirement might seem like nothing more than a vague concept to you. Meanwhile, in the here and now, the thought of driving a shiny new car is much more appealing than saving money for some distant dream.

But, by following just three simple rules, you will save a substantial amount of money in this area of your finances; and those three rules are to buy used, never finance for more than three years, and keep every vehicle for at least five years after you pay off the loan.

These rules, however, as simple as they are, can be a real test of your self-discipline when it comes to facing up to the constant bombardment of the auto industry as they push their wares. They spend millions of dollars every year to spread the gospel of the SUV and Hummer!

And where does the money come from to pay for all that advertising? Well, if you buy what they're selling, some part of it will come right out of your pocket.

I fell for their siren-song when I was younger; it is a mistake many of us make. The good news is that the day you change your buying habits is the day your recovery will begin. Having a car is a practical accommodation in modern life; the trick to money well saved is to get where you're going while, at the same time, making room in your budget for financial peace of mind.

Chapter Twenty-Nine

More Car Talk

It is your own conviction that compels you—
choice compels choice.

—Epictetus

Now, there are some financial pundits who would advise you to save and pay cash every time you purchase a vehicle. But I don't believe that is the best financial move unless and until all your other financial goals have been achieved. And, even then, you should carefully weigh your other options.

Yes, you will pay interest on a car loan, but when you pay cash you will lose the interest that money could have been earning if you had not spent it on the car (or truck, SUV, whatever). When you spend money on one thing, you lose the opportunity to spend it somewhere else; that is what is known as *opportunity cost*.

And, when you spend money, you also lose the opportunity to save that money, instead. This is important, so let me explain this statement in more detail.

No money is more expensive than the money you spend today because it stops the power of compounded interest. No less a mind than Albert Einstein called compound interest the eighth wonder of the world and the greatest mathematical discovery of all time! Pretty strong words for the guy who put together $E=MC^2$.

Nothing will enhance your peace of mind quite like money in the bank and, when you choose to spend when you could have saved, you also surrender that same amount of ready-cash liquidity, which you will wish you had if the need ever arises.

If it is time for you to make a vehicle purchase, I recommend you consider a mid-range, low-mileage used car that is in good condition and at least three years old. A car like that will save you as much as fifty percent of its original purchase price and cost somewhere between eight and twelve thousand dollars.

Certainly, that figure represents a substantial savings but it is still a lot of money! And I don't believe it is the best financial decision you can make to choose to have that amount of cash tied up in a depreciating asset. And it is a really bad idea if you have any unsecured debt or don't have an Income Emergency Fund.

In fact, I would rather see it drawing interest in a CD even if all your other financial ducks are in a row and even if you are paying more in interest on the loan than you are earning on the money in the bank. Why? Well, a couple of reasons. One, the money will always be there in case of an emergency. And, two, the money will always be there in case of an emergency.

When, instead, you sink ready-cash into a vehicle purchase and you suddenly need the money, you might have to sell the car and be forced to somehow do without. Not only that but, in that situation, you might have to sell the car for less than it is actually worth in order to cash out as quickly as possible!

If you don't have the money in your budget to support a loan payment but you do have the money to pay cash, you might consider depositing the money in a long-term, interest bearing account like a money-market account, for example, and making the payment from the balance of that account. By doing so, you reduce the total amount of interest you pay while still maintaining the maximum amount of cash liquidity.

Sure, you're going to pay some interest on the loan but it will be worth it to maintain a more positive financial position and a higher level of cash liquidity. And, if you shop smart for both the vehicle and the loan, the difference between the interest the money earns and what you are paying can be kept to a minimum.

A final consideration in weighing your financial options when it comes to paying cash or financing a vehicle purchase is, what I call, the *endowment factor*.

Most major universities and many large charitable foundations finance some portion of their operations using proceeds from, what is known as, an endowment. An endowment, for our purposes, can be thought of as a certain type of savings account. The amount of an endowment for a major university, for example, can run into the billions of dollars and it will earn millions of dollars of interest—year after year!

But what is important for you to know is that any institution that does use the interest proceeds from an endowment to finance their operations will avoid ever spending any of the principal of that endowment. In fact, they always plan to spend less every year than the total amount of the interest they expect to earn in that year because, by doing so, the size of the endowment will continue to grow.

Does that sound familiar to you? It should because that is the exact strategy encompassed by my plan to continually grow your margin. The financial-types who make a living managing large endowments are among the sharpest tools in the shed, so pay attention to how they manage that money. And you should follow their example to the extent that you consider your savings as your personal endowment and *never* spend the principal.

There is a story told about a man who is shunned by everyone in his ultra-conservative community. When an outsider asks one of the locals why, he is told, simply, "he dipped into his capital."

Money is hard to come by and, while spending your savings should not make you a pariah in your community, you should always be reluctant to let go of it too easily or when it is not absolutely necessary that you do so. That is not to imply that you should be miserly but, rather, that you spend smartly. You can probably find better uses for your money than locking up big chunks of it in a depreciating asset, such as a vehicle.

In fact, in Step Seven, we will discuss financial independence as the ultimate state of financial peace of mind. Financial independence is achieved by replacing income from work with income from interest on savings (not investments because you can't count on the return from investments in the short-term).

It will be your personal endowment, that is, the total amount you have saved and that is earning you interest, that will provide you with the income you need to achieve financial independence.

The sooner you get money into your endowment and growing, the better. So, instead of paying cash for a vehicle, make a down payment that will be just enough to make the payments on a three-year loan fit well within your budget and put the rest to work—forever—in a personal endowment of your own. That is how the great universities do it, that is how the wealthy do it, and that is how you should do it too!

In the following section, Step Five, you will learn a way to budget that will use the power of your margin to make yourself virtually debt-proof.

STEP FIVE

Reserve Your Peace

Chapter Thirty

Make Yourself Debt-Proof

There is no somewhere, there is only the road to
somewhere and we are always on it.

—David Campbell

Money can become a real pain in the neck if you let it but, the thing is, the pain does not always begin with any conscious decision on your part to overspend. It can start with something as innocent as overlooking a few of your actual costs of living.

The idea of settling your debts and the benefits of living debt-free are not unfamiliar to most of us. The concept of being debt-proof, however, is not all that common, so let me explain the term for you as I use it.

A major cause of debt and financial upset is the failure to account for all of our actual costs of living. Even if we manage our finances using a budget, some of our expenses simply escape us and, so, go unaccounted for until they actually come due.

When you let that happen, that is, when you fail to account for all your expenses, the effects of doing so can cascade through your entire financial life. The problem is that not all of your expenses are all that easy to deal with unless and until you learn how to do so.

A few years ago, I suffered my own financial setback and as part of my recovery I began using a budget for the first time in my life. What I soon learned is that learning to use a budget effectively was like learning any other skill—it takes time. One of the issues I encountered was how to account for bills and other expenses that came due on some schedule other than monthly.

The other problem I had when I was learning to budget was how to plan for the bills that seemed to pop up sort of unexpected-like. I say *unexpected-like* because they weren't exactly out-of-the-blue, they were more like coming at me from out of left field. For example, I knew that I would *probably* have some sort of dental emergency once or twice a year but, then again, maybe not if I got lucky.

How do you budget for something like that? Well, I finally figured it out after a few dead-ends and false starts. And, later, when I was teaching financial management, I learned that others were facing the same issues.

One cost that often goes unconsidered in our monthly budgeting is the fact that everyday every *thing* we own is wearing out to one extent or another and will, eventually, need to be replaced if it is something we can't live without.

Take, for example, the tires on your car (or truck or SUV, whatever). Every time you drive your car, the tires experience some wear and that wear is adding up. Now, you can choose to ignore that wear but eventually, it is a bill that will come due. And, when it does, the question then is: will you be ready for it?

I have often been asked how to budget for *unexpected* expenses. Most often, my response is that there are very few expenses that are actually unexpected. Certainly, tires wearing out and the fact that they will someday need to be replaced can hardly be defined as unexpected. That is what tires do—they wear out!

Likewise, the clock on every appliance you own is ticking because you know that not one of them will last forever. The same thing is also happening to the car you drive—it's wearing out. And our clothes are going out of style and our shoes seem destined for that great cobbler in the sky all too soon. The TV could go any day and who knows when a tooth will begin to ache! Time and use both take a toll on all our *stuff* and that toll is a bill that will eventually come due.

So none of the examples mentioned fall into the category of an *unexpected* expense. But they are costs that are difficult to account for (until you know how) and easy to overlook and, so, are often not being adequately planned for in our monthly spending. The only way to do that, to address these kinds of expenses, is, first, to budget and, second, to include a line item in that budget meant specifically to fund them when they come due.

We all know that expenses like these are bound to happen, even if it is not entirely possible to know when, exactly, they will come due. But ignoring these expenses by failing to adequately plan for them is another way many of us increase the level of financial stress in our lives.

Unexpected expenses are not really unexpected. Unexpected expenses are really expenses that we fail to plan for and they can often be that proverbial last straw that can break our financial back because, when an unplanned for expense does comes along, we have only a few options for coming up with the money we need; none of which are conducive to financial peace of mind.

One option you have is to simply not pay it. This might even be a viable option if it's something you can live without. Another option will be to find the money somewhere else in your budget. Unfortunately, this could result in some other bill (or bills!) going unpaid. When you exercise this option, you end up juggling bills and it is often a circus act that can last for months as you struggle to catch-up.

The name given to this second option is robbing Peter to pay Paul and, although it is an option, it is almost never a good idea. And, finally, the third option that might be available is to borrow the money to meet the expense. This is probably the most popular option and the way most of us deal with the issue when it comes up.

And this, then, is how our, so-called, money troubles usually begin. An expense that goes unplanned for is like the first domino in a long line that, once it is tipped, goes on to take down all the others. Borrowing is often the first step to a financial meltdown and it can be the beginning of the end because borrowed money will need to be repaid.

First of all, let's call *borrowed* money by its real name— credit! And what credit usually translates to in the real world is charging the bill to one credit card or another. But when you use credit to compensate for inadequate planning it can often be the start of that same cycle of overspending and debt addressed in Step Four.

When you add to your debt load to cover budget shortfalls the result will be that the money to pay the bill on that new debt will need to come from somewhere else in your budget. It is finding that money that can be the problem, particularly if you are already overspending or living paycheck to paycheck.

And, then, when the next unplanned for expense comes along, whether it's a toothache that is going to need a root canal and crown or the tires that give up the ghost, a tight budget can get even tighter. You can see where this can lead over time, right?

Usually, it will lead right back to the plastic and yet more debt. And, then, it's yet another bill or a higher amount to accommodate in your already tight budget. It is a vicious and self-perpetuating cycle. Your peace of mind can't help but be affected in a negative way when you are always living in dread of the next financial surprise you just know is coming!

The good news is that you can, in fact, plan for these kinds of expenses. They don't have to take you by surprise or find you unprepared. You can manage your finances so that you are, in fact, prepared to meet these expenses each and every time they come due, even if you don't know exactly when that will be.

Chapter Thirty-One

Accounting For What Goes Unaccounted For

*Things which matter most must never be at the
mercy of things that matter least.*

—Goethe

Each of the seven steps is, basically, a fundamental of
sound money management, if with something less than an
entirely conventional attitude. Spending thoughtfully, having a
plan to save, maintaining a certain amount of cash liquidity, and
living debt-free are each simply good ideas when it comes to
managing your money.

But unless you identify *all* your actual costs and, then,
budget to meet each and every one of them, achieving financial
peace of mind is likely to prove elusive. When you do not
identify all your expenses, you are almost certain to overspend
and the money you think you are saving will be an illusion.

When we *are* in a position to meet each and every cost
associated with supporting our lifestyle, then, and only then, can
true financial peace of mind be realized.

The fact is that most of us underestimate our actual cost of living. Let's reconsider that tire example I used in the last chapter: Every mile you drive is depreciating the asset your tires represent but how many of us prorate the cost of new tires on a monthly basis?

And take that other example I used about the washing machine. Again, we all know that a washing machine will last about ten years or so, but unless we budget for its replacement over its useful life we will be unprepared when it dies and the dirty clothes are piling up.

But those sorts of costs are only one example of costs that often get overlooked and unaccounted for in an otherwise well-intentioned budget. Bills that come due on some schedule other than monthly are also the cause of a lot of unnecessary financial distress. Real estate property taxes and car insurance are just two examples of these sorts of non-monthly but recurring expenses.

Certainly, you could meet these unplanned for expenses with the money in your emergency fund, assuming it is sufficient, but that is not what that fund is for. Remember, the recurring and actual costs associated with our lifestyle are not financial emergencies. Your emergency fund is your fallback position in the case of a real emergency; in particular, it is your protection against unemployment.

And, when savings are used to cover regular expenses, they aren't really savings, are they? Instead of dipping into your emergency fund to compensate for a lack of planning, better planning is what is actually required to address the issue. And, those costs and expenses that don't fit neatly into a monthly budget format are, in fact, readily addressed using, what I call, a *Reserve Account*.

I call them "Reserve Accounts" because that is what they are—money put aside and held in *reserve* for expenses that are bound to arrive, even if we don't know exactly when the bill will come due. They are also handy tools that you can use to manage other aspects of your spending, as well, but their primary purpose is to act as a place-holder in your monthly budget.

The first thing you need to do is identify those costs that you have overlooked in the past and that are presently going unaccounted for in your budget. I have already mentioned a couple, tires and medical bills, but those are just two examples and there are likely to be others. I recommend that you dig through your financial records for the last two years or so in order to ferret them out.

An easy way to begin the process of identifying these expenses will be to review a years worth of checking and charge card statements. For example, take medical expenses not covered by health insurance. If a review of your records shows that over the last twelve months you spent $600 in this category, you simply divide that number by twelve to arrive at the prorated, monthly cost of this expense, $50.

Now, you need a place to keep this money. Your regular checking account won't work and neither will your savings account. If you put your Reserve Account funds into either of those accounts, it is too hard to keep them separate and they are likely to be spent.

The answer, then, is to open a second checking account just for your Reserve Account deposits, what I call your *Reserve Checking Account* and that is where you deposit the $50 you're putting away every month to meet medical expenses.

With your Reserve Account in place and the money in your Reserve Checking Account, when an expense pops up you won't need to rob Peter to pay Paul or resort to charging it on a credit card. All you do is write a check for it out of your Reserve Checking Account. And, when *all* of your costs are accounted for in this way, you will be debt-proof. You will have largely eliminated the element of surprise from your financial life.

Reserve Accounts are like instant karma or something! Before Reserve Accounts you would probably curse your luck when the battery in your car died. Now, with money in the bank, it is no big deal—all you do is write the check and forget about it! Nothing will change your financial luck for the better like better accounting!

The obvious problem with using Reserve Accounts is that it takes money to fund them. And that money will be hard to come by if your budget is already tight. But the fact is that funding these accounts is not an option. I mean, think about it— if you don't have the money to save every month to replace your tires when they wear out, where will the money come from when the bill comes due?

It reminds me of a line from a commercial—you can pay me now or you can pay me later! And we all know that the "pay-me-later" road leads, almost always, to debt and stress.

Working with Reserve Accounts does take some practice. And it is likely to take you some time to find the money to fund all of the Reserve Accounts for which you identify a need.

As you begin to implement the strategies covered in Steps One, Two, and Three, less of your income will go to pay the bills so more will be available to save. At first, however, it probably won't be enough to fund more than two or three Reserve Accounts. But that will give you time to develop your skills in using Reserve Accounts.

The trick, at first, is to identify those two or three bills that always seem to catch you unprepared and set up a Reserve Account to fund each of them.

For example, car insurance is a common example of a bill we all have but most us are only billed once or twice a year for it. So, how would you account for that in a monthly budget? All you do is divide the total of the annual amount by twelve to arrive at the monthly amount and that is the amount you would deposit every month to your Reserve Account to pay the bill when it comes due.

Think about that for a minute and think about what is happening in one situation compared to the other. In the typical, caught unprepared scenario, you are scrambling for the money and frustrated with your own lack of financial planning. On the other hand, when you have budgeted to pay the bill whenever it comes due, the money will be there waiting in your Reserve Account.

Chapter Thirty-Two

The Mechanics of Living Debt-Proof

*Sometimes when I consider what tremendous
consequences come from little things, I am
tempted to think that there are no little things.*

—Bruce Barton

You will need to keep track of the balance in each
individual Reserve Account on a monthly basis but you don't
need a separate checking account for each of them. You will
deposit the monthly total of all your individual Reserve
Accounts into a single checking account, your Reserve Checking
Account, and you will pay any Reserve Account expense with
money from that account.

For example, let's say you start with three Reserve
Accounts and that each is funded every month with the following
amounts:

Car Insurance	$50
Auto Expenses	$25
Gifts	$35

That means that, every month, you would deposit the total of these amounts, $110, to your Reserve Checking Account. You can keep track of the total amount of your Reserve Checking Account using the checkbook register you got when you opened that account but you will also need to account for the balance in each of your individual Reserve Accounts. The way you do that is by keeping an individual register for each of them.

Those individual registers work just like any checkbook register, that is, you enter your beginning balance, add deposits, and subtract withdrawals. Here is an example of what the register for the Reserve Checking Account would look like using the numbers from the previous example:

Date	Transaction Details	Withdrawal	Deposit	Balance
3/1	Monthly Funding		$110	$400
4/1	Monthly Funding		$110	$510
4/3	Auto Expenses/Battery	$75		$435
5/1	Monthly Funding		$110	$545
5/13	Gift/JB Birthday	$45		$500

As you can see, each time a payment is made, you would include the name of the Reserve Account from which the withdrawal for that payment was made. I also add a brief description of the expense in this register and put a more detailed description of the expense in the register of the respective Reserve Account.

I keep the register for each of my Reserve Accounts on an individual sheet of lined notebook paper. Each of those sheets I keep in a three-ring binder. I never have bothered to computerize the process even though I'm usually keeping around six or seven (or more!) individual Reserve Accounts at any one time. Exactly how you do it, however, is not as important as actually using Reserve Accounts to gain more control of your spending!

Like learning to manage your finances using a monthly budget, you will get better at working with Reserve Accounts over time. Also, it is quite possible that an expense will come up for which the balance of the individual Reserve Account is insufficient. This is most likely to occur when you first begin funding an account.

The easy way to avoid this from happening is to fund an account with three or four months of funding up front, although, I know this will not always be an option. If you have sufficient savings, you might consider using that money to "front-load" one or more Reserve Accounts.

Also, after a few months of funding your Reserve Accounts, the balance will begin to grow and could become quite substantial. Some accounts, those in which you incur few or, even, no expenses for a number of months can grow to an amount larger than is likely to ever be needed.

This is what happened in my Reserve Account for medical expenses. I went through a couple of years without any major expenses and the account grew to exceed the amount of what is called the annual catastrophic limit. That limit is the amount at which I no longer have to pay any deductible for covered services. Once I had that amount, however, I did not quit contributing to that account.

Instead, what I did was lower the amount of the monthly funding and, at the end of every year, I use any amount remaining in that account to fund a negative balance in some other account or, simply, add it to savings. If you do find yourself with an account that has a large annual surplus, it could mean that you should consider lowering the amount of your monthly contribution.

You never want to eliminate a Reserve Account as long as it is an expense that needs to be accounted for but you might consider combining some smaller individual expenses into a single account. I have a Reserve Account I use this way and it helps to reduce the number of individual accounts I need to keep track of.

Chapter Thirty-Three

The Art of Debt-Proofing

*Plan for the future because that is where you are
going to spend the rest of your life.*

—Mark Twain

Reserve Accounts are also a great tool for budgeting that spending that does need to be controlled or otherwise managed but does not fit readily into your spending plan. Take the money you spend on gifts, for example. Most of us just buy gifts using whatever money we have available. The money spent on gifts can really add up though, especially if we are not keeping track of the total and, even then, if we are spending without some sort of a limit.

We actually have quite a few spending categories where the same sort of controls would help us to manage our spending, clothes being one that most of us are familiar with. Unless we have established a monthly allowance for these items in our budget, it is too easy to spend more than we intended and even more than we can afford.

A Reserve Account can help you to avoid both of those spending traps. For example, let's say you want to spend no more than $1,200 a year on buying new clothes. That works out to $100 a month and this is the amount you would deposit each month to the Reserve Account named—guess what?—Clothes!

Here is where a very interesting aspect of Reserve Account funding can come into play. In continuing with the previous example, let's say you have a couple of months of funding your four Reserve Accounts (car insurance, car expenses, gifts, and, now, clothes) under your belt and the total in those accounts and in your Reserve Checking Account is $420.

Now, let's say, you find a suit on sale for $300 but the register for your clothes account shows the balance to be only $200. You can actually *borrow* from the $420 balance and buy the suit anyway, as long as you realize that any further clothes purchases will need to be curtailed until the other accounts are paid back.

The ability to *borrow* between Reserve Accounts is one of their most appealing features but, as attractive as it is, it must be used with great care and planning to avoid bad timing. When you borrow from one account or accounts for another, you need to be sure it won't leave you short for a bill that is coming due.

If your borrowing leaves you with $120 remaining in your Reserve Checking Account and next months funding brings the total to $330 but you have a $350 automobile insurance payment due that month, you have over-borrowed. That is why I pointed out earlier that getting good at working with Reserve Accounts will take some time and practice.

It will also help to avoid over-borrowing if you keep a calendar that shows when Reserve Account bills are coming due and that, when you do borrow, you keep that schedule in mind.

Of course, this only applies to those bills that actually have a due date. It is not always prudent to borrow from those Reserve Accounts for expenses that happen when they happen, like a dental emergency.

Also, you can actually plan to borrow and not pay the borrowed amount back if you think the remaining balance in the account from which you borrowed is large enough for its intended purpose.

Reserve Accounts are also a good way to make your dreams come true. Our dreams are important and it is important to keep your dreams alive. The best way to keep a dream alive is to know that you are moving towards making it a reality; take a dream to see Paris in the spring, for example.

If all you do is dream about it, it is unlikely to ever come to pass. Of course, we can always charge the trip to a credit card but that can lead to feelings of guilt during the trip, remorse afterwards, and the hangover of debt for years to come. A better way to realize the dream is simply to budget for it using a Reserve Account.

If you figure the trip will cost $3,000 and you want to take it two years from now, all you do is divide the total cost by the number of months you have to get it funded by your target date. $3,000 divided by 24 months equals $125 a month. If you don't have that amount in your budget, you now have the information you need to rearrange your finances.

Either you reduce expenses elsewhere, if your dream is that compelling for you, or you extend your deadline from twenty-four months to, say, thirty months. Or you get a second job or work overtime, whatever, you now can exercise some real planning when it comes to achieving your dreams!

What before your Reserve Account was only a vague, unformed idea floating around in your head, is now a goal on its way to being realized. Before you had a hope, now you have a date to start packing!

So, now that you are more familiar with the concept of being debt-proof and you have been introduced to using Reserve Accounts as an advanced but fundamental budgeting tool, we can move on to the next section—Step Six. In Step Six, you will be introduced to a method for securing your most valuable possession, your home, in a way that is a bit unorthodox and that also serves to keep your personal endowment growing and maximize your liquidity.

STEP SIX

Unscramble Your Nest Egg

Chapter Thirty-Four

Home By Another Way

Our house is a very, very, very fine house.

—Crosby, Stills and Nash

A house is just so much glass and wood but that collection of building materials, arranged just so, can become a home and our own sacred ground. But the human race has come relatively of late to the whole idea of home as we know it today and for millions of years we were mostly small nomadic tribes wandering a hostile landscape.

It was the *invention* of agriculture that allowed us to plant our own roots and the notion of "place" was born. And, almost as soon as the individual tribes settled, we began to associate with our place. We became, then, in part, where we were *from*. Now, our place is a part of who we *are*; it defines us in a way we have all come to understand and it is how we identify ourselves.

We are *Canadians* or *Russians* or *Americans* or whatever our place is named and, then, we are also Texans or

Californians or whatever. But our desire to define our place does not end there and it is not enough for someone from New York City to say that they are from New York City. A New Yorker is from the Bronx or Queens, Soho, Noho, Harlem or any one of the many other distinctive neighborhoods.

Our place of origin remains with us even after we have left and our roots have been planted elsewhere. We go back, when we can, to visit the old neighborhood and see old friends. We hold reunions and the disparate parts gather and reassemble as family.

And when we gather it is often within the familiar walls of the home of our parents; the one place that will always be home even if we now have homes we call our own.

These are just a few of the sentiments of home but there are, of course, as many as individual memories exist. But as individual as they are, we are also of a collective consciousness and we share many meanings for the word *home*. And the physical embodiment that is the container of that consciousness, we call a house.

And, so, a house can be much more than just so many walls and a roof. A house can become a home and a home can become a hallowed space. In that sense, our home can occupy both a spiritual and physical place in our life and, because it is *special* in this way, our home deserves special consideration in our financial planning.

But in our country the concept of home is still evolving. The USA is becoming a more and more mobile society and this increased mobility is becoming reflected in how we deem to house ourselves. We are more likely now to move more often than the previous generation and several times in our lives. We are more likely to own several homes during our lifetime and become serial home owners.

The younger we are, the shorter our stays, on average, in any one place. We move from place to place, state to state, and city to city and all this moving means that the concept must be more moveable as well. We have gone back to the future, in some sense, and becoming more nomadic after being less so for a long time.

All this mobility has come with a price, however. On average, we stay in a house only about seven years and the mortgage of choice in an inflating real estate market has become the thirty year mortgage. And it is often the case that each time we change houses, we begin again with a new thirty year mortgage with a higher initial balance than before.

The *old* society, where people and jobs were much more stable, has morphed into a culture where we move and change jobs, place, and housing much more frequently.

Owning a home outright, mortgage-free, was once a basic step on the way to retirement. Now, even if we are lucky enough to be able to retire, a mortgage will often be a part of that retirement. This change is a reflection of the fact that moving and resettling is an expensive proposition and it also speaks of a new economy where already inflated housing prices continue to soar.

But, even if owning a home mortgage-free is a financial strategy with its roots in the old economy, there can be no denying that having a mortgage makes retiring that much more expensive. In fact, it can even make or break the entire proposition. The question, then, is how do we get there from *here*?

In the old economy, housing represented a smaller percentage of our income simply because houses cost so much less. Now, in the new economy, home prices have forced adaptations in the mortgage industry. In the old economy, twenty year mortgages were the norm, now they have been replaced by mortgages of thirty years or more.

We can all understand that the longer the term of a loan the more interest we will pay but, because we owe more at the beginning of a loan than at the end, we pay much more interest at the beginning, as well.

To understand this dynamic, a thirty-year mortgage is best considered as six five-year blocks. On average, during the first five-year block, only a small percentage of your mortgage payment is applied towards paying down the principal. That first five-year block is the most expensive money you are likely to ever borrow in your life!

The percentage of your total payment applied to principal varies with each five-year block and that percentage is higher the further you are into the mortgage. To illustrate that point, the following is the average percentages that apply for a thirty year mortgage with an any interest rate between about six and twelve percent during each of the six five-year blocks:

Years	% Applied to Principal	% Applied to Interest
1 – 5	5	95
6 – 10	9	91
11 – 15	15	85
16 – 20	26	74
21 – 25	44	56
26 – 30	77	23

Those numbers reveal the dark side of home financing. For one thing, it shows just how little equity you buy for your money in the first ten years of a thirty year mortgage. Why this is important is that, if we are moving every seven years and starting all over with a new thirty year mortgage each time we resettle, we will never make any progress towards retiring our mortgage.

And the numbers in that chart also reveal just how expensive a thirty year mortgage is; even if you manage to stay put, you will end up paying an amount equal to almost three times the original cost of your house. Think about that for a moment and think about what a house can cost these days. Is that money well spent or not?

New realities aside, I don't think so but, as I said, the thirty year mortgage came about because of rising real estate prices in many parts of the country. Extending the term of the loan was the only way many people could afford to buy a house and it still serves that function today. But that does not necessarily mean that taking thirty years to pay off your mortgage is a sound financial strategy.

Chapter Thirty-Five

The Myth of a Rising Tide

Don't it make you wanna go home, now, don't it
make you wanna go home.

—Joe South

The necessity of thirty-year mortgages aside, it is, nevertheless, only prudent to build equity in our home. And, even in light of the way people and jobs move around these days, you can still do that; it is just that the Old Economy strategy of becoming mortgage-free by retirement needs to be adapted to the realities of a more moveable society and an inflated and inflating housing market.

The mantra of the New Economy housing market is that appreciation will bail us out. And our politicians took a major step in promoting this ethic when they made it possible to cash out your home equity, tax-free, every two years.

The law that made that possible is the New Economy equivalent of the carrot and stick because, as long as we keep moving and prices keep going up, we are not making any real progress. It is, what I call, The Myth of a Rising Tide.

Let's look at the financial reality of a $250,000 mortgage at eight percent interest. There is a handy tool called a remaining balance table that will help us with our analysis. Referring to that tool, it shows that, after five years, the remaining balance on that mortgage amount and at that eight percent interest will be .9507 or $237,675.

This means that five years of mortgage payments have bought you $12,325 of equity. But is the total of your mortgage payments all you have spent on your home over that time? No way, right? You will have spent a lot more than that because owning a house incurs all sorts of other expenses including property taxes, homeowners insurance, and maintenance.

If, for the sake of example, we assume that these other costs are equal to five percent of the purchase price per year (and, on average, they will) this adds another $12,500 a year to the total annual mortgage payment of $22,013 for a combined annual total of more than $34,500.

Over five years, then, you will have spent a total of $172,565.50 to *buy* a measly $12,000 in equity. But what about appreciation, you ask? In order to just breakeven, the house will need to have appreciated by seventy percent! That amounts to a sustained average annual appreciation rate of about ten percent over those five years, not counting the costs of selling, buying and moving.

But even if you meet or exceed that rate of appreciation, that appreciation will not actually be realized if you buy into another market that has experienced appreciation at the same rate or higher. If you cash out with $175,000 in gains and take that gain into a comparable housing market, replacing the home you just sold will now cost you at least $425,000. And because your maintenance, taxes and insurance will be higher than before, you will have actually lost ground.

What that means is that your gains are not just gone but that they were an illusion to begin with. If Congress had not acted to exempt appreciation from taxes, far fewer of us would be able to afford the cost of serial home ownership.

And do you think the politicians acted out of the goodness of their hearts? Well, in fact, they did it because the housing industry lobbied hard and paid big money to get the tax laws changed to perpetuate The Myth. If they had not, the housing market boom of the nineties that has continued into the new millennium would have stalled out years ago.

The only way that appreciation is actually realized is when you either down-scale dramatically or drop out of the market altogether. The only time that happens, usually, is in retirement.

But even in a changing society and a New Economy, building equity is as important to your financial peace of mind as it has ever been. The question, then, is how do you unscramble your nest egg?

Chapter Thirty-Six

Gurus to Go

You don't need a weatherman to know which
way the wind blows.

—Bob Dylan

Financial advice comes and financial advice goes. The money guru of the day always has his or her own words of wisdom that might or might not make sense for you, your particular financial situation, and your personal financial goals.

But one problem with guru-speak is that their advise must be as generic as possible and directed at the broadest possible market. While you, on the other hand, have very specific ends you want to accomplish.

Another problem you will encounter when looking for financial guidance is that many of the pundits contradict each other. Take the issue at hand, for example, home ownership. Some of the gurus advise you "invest" in your mortgage by accelerating your payments to principal ahead of the mortgage repayment schedule. By paying ahead of schedule, they say, you will payoff your mortgage sooner and save on interest.

On the other hand, there are those who will tell you that the smart move is to take that money and invest in the stock market, instead, because the odds are you will realize a higher return.

Well, maybe you will and maybe you won't but, I'll tell you something—nothing will add to your feeling of financial well-being and security quite like paying off your mortgage. Yes, there are other investments "out there" that *might* provide a slightly higher return than investing in your mortgage, but only the stock market has actually *averaged* a comparable return over the last fifty years.

But the stock market is not a sure thing in the short term while the income that previously went to making the mortgage payment, once your mortgage is paid off, is money in the bank and just that certain. If that money had, instead, been *invested* in the stock market, your outcome is absolutely in question.

The market advocates preach the sermon of the long term, but, as has been said before, over the long term we are all dead. During market downturns it is difficult to think *long term* as you watch your balance steadily declining, particularly, if you count on dividends for income.

Money you definitely don't have to spend is more soothing than money that might or might not be coming in. In addition to the fact that paying off your mortgage is a *sure thing*, it just feels good. And, then, there is the simple fact that the longer you take to pay off your mortgage the more you are paying to acquire the asset your home represents.

If you finance a $100,000 home purchase over thirty years, at a fixed mortgage interest rate of eight percent or so, you will pay approximately 2.65 times the original amount of the loan or about $265,000. Even if you cut the term of a mortgage to twenty years, you will still pay more than twice the original amount of the loan.

The exact amount of the total you will spend will depend on your interest rate but does it ever make sense to you to pay two or almost three times its original cost for something? No, it does not and it is one thing when you are talking about something that cost ten, one-hundred or, even, one-thousand dollars; it is quite another when what you are paying for costs as much as homes do these days!

And, remember, we're not talking about a few bucks here. The sooner you pay off your mortgage the sooner that income that previously went to mortgage payments is available to go towards further securing your financial future instead of interest which adds nothing to your bottom line!

A smart approach to home ownership begins with the mortgage, itself. Again, the first two five year blocks of a thirty year mortgage buy you almost nothing but time. The problem is that many of us will need a thirty year mortgage in order to bring the payments down enough so that we can qualify for the mortgage in the first place.

A twenty year mortgage is always a better option, if you can afford it. If not, the next best alternative is to plan to leave those first two blocks behind you as soon as possible.

The actual process of retiring your mortgage on whatever schedule meets your available income is as simple as sending in whatever extra amount you can afford with each payment but it is better that you have a *thoughtful* plan to retire your mortgage.

To do that, to retire your mortgage thoughtfully, will mean that you understand the effect and consequences of one action compared to another. For example, on a fixed rate mortgage, adding enough to your monthly payment to equal to another full monthly payment every year will reduce a thirty-year mortgage by over seven years. And you will save yourself over $45,000 on each $100,000 of mortgage—almost fifty percent!

And, not only that, you will also reclaim the opportunity cost that you lose when you don't have that income free to invest elsewhere. Remember, you have a lot to accomplish with your money, tying it up it mortgage payments might be necessary but you still want to free it up as soon as possible.

One of the common arguments against paying off one's mortgage is that you lose the tax write-off. Anyone who makes this argument is either uninformed or being disingenuous to bolster the case for other investments.

When you deduct mortgage interest from your taxes, the actual *net* savings is equal to the taxes you would pay on an equivalent amount of income. If you had $10,000 in deductions and your average tax rate was twenty percent, you would end up paying $2,000 less in taxes but end up with $8,000 less in your pocket. In other words, it will *cost* you eighty cents to avoid twenty cents in taxes.

Another argument made against early mortgage retirement is that the money repaid on a long-term loan, such as a mortgage, is worth less as time passes because it is devalued due to inflation and so it saves today's more valuable dollars to delay repayment as long as possible.

Again, there is another financial side to that argument. The sooner you are able to save money that previously went to mortgage payments, the more valuable *those* dollars are because the sooner you will be able to put that money to work earning interest and the longer the power of compounded interest will have to work its magic.

One final argument against investing in your mortgage is that equity is difficult to access in case of an emergency. Actually, I think, that argues in favor of equity investing. After all, do you really want your most valuable asset to be too easily encumbered? And, besides, the availability of home equity lines of credit totally discredits this argument.

Also, there's the fact that one of the seven steps addresses this very issue. In Chapter Three the benefits of an emergency fund are covered and, hopefully, before the need arises your fund will be in place. If not, you still have options that would make better financial sense than borrowing against your home.

But, again, investing in equity needs to be approached in the same thoughtful manner that I advocate for spending of any sort. And the ground we covered in Step One, that advises you to spend with a purpose, still applies.

In fact, thoughtful spending is never more important than when dealing with a mortgage simply because the dollar amounts are so large and, consequently, the stakes so high.

Chapter Thirty-Seven

Homeward Bound

To everything there is a season, a time for every purpose under the sun.

—Ecclesiastes 3:1

To every thing there *is* a season and this applies to your financial life as well as to life in general. Owning a home is a big responsibility and not one to be undertaken lightly. The first consideration when planning for home ownership should be your own plans for the future and your lifestyle.

Even in an appreciating market, it is seldom a good financial decision to enter into a mortgage if you plan to move in five years or less. If you plan to live where you are for any period of time over five years, and if you are so inclined, you could possibly build equity and, so, profit by buying instead of renting a place to live.

However, that profit can be an illusion if, when you do move, it is to a housing market where the prices are about the same or higher. In that case, all you will have done is managed to stay even—maybe! But, then again, maybe not; not when you also subtract all the *true* costs associated with moving from whatever profit you might gross.

Many people forget just how expensive moving can be and it will seldom prove to be conducive to your peace of mind. Moving can be an adventure and living somewhere new can be exciting but, even if you move for a better paying job, you can lose money by moving in more ways than one.

If you are moving for the excitement of it and to experience new places, renting is almost always a better option, financially. The argument that renting is throwing away your money is simply wrong. There is a value to having a place to live and when you rent what you are doing is paying for that value.

And, besides, owning a home is almost always more expensive even over the long-term. If, and this is a big if, you were to rent and save the difference between renting and owning (and I mean *all* the costs), your savings would be likely to equal any *real* appreciation you might realize. The problem is that most of us would spend the difference not bank it!

Also, owning a home can fix a portion of our cost of housing, assuming a fixed rate mortgage, and that can help us beat inflation but that advantage is lost every time we move. And, besides, owning a home involves many more headaches and expenses than does renting so it is hard to compare apples with apples in that equation.

So, if you need to retain a high degree of mobility, buying should not be your first priority. If, however, you do plan to stay where you are for at least five years, you might consider buying. Spending smartly when you buy a home begins with not overspending your income—the fundamental lesson of the Seven Steps. And here is the hard light of the truth of things—you cannot afford a thirty year loan.

A thirty year loan is simply too expensive. The better strategy is to first determine how much house you qualify for with a twenty year mortgage and confine your looking to that price range. If there is nothing in that price range and you choose to go with a thirty year mortgage, regardless, the next best strategy is prepay principal to move you out of that first ten year period as soon as you can afford to do so.

An easy way to determine that point is to look at the mortgage payment schedule. This schedule is usually provided with your loan documentation. You can also find these on the internet, as well. The mortgage payment schedule shows you how much of each of your monthly payments goes to principal and how much to interest. It also shows the balance at the end of each scheduled payment.

All you need to do, once you have the payment schedule for your mortgage, is to determine what the balance will be at the end of year ten and subtract that amount from the present balance. The amount that results from doing so is the amount you want to prepay as soon as possible in order to get past that first ten year block as fast as you can.

This figure, basically, represents what it cost you buy those extra ten years of financing that made your home affordable for you. The problem is that the reason you got a thirty year mortgage in the first place was because it was all you could afford, so where will you get the extra to pay towards accelerating the principal reduction?

The money will come from your rising income and following The Fifty Percent Plan, of course. As soon as you have you your emergency fund in place, those savings should be used to buy back the time you financed using a thirty year mortgage. Mortgage money during the first ten years of a thirty year mortgage is much more expensive than credit card debt will ever be!

The average credit card debt in the USA is about $8,400 with an average interest rate of 18.9%, according to Consumer Credit Counseling. That means if you don't pay a dime of principal over a year's time, the total amount of interest you would pay would be about $750. The average amount of interest paid per $100,000 of mortgage at just six percent interest (less than one-third of the interest rate on the credit card debt in this example) will be $3,660 a year—almost five times as much!

This will be a new perspective to many people and a case of not seeing the forest for the financial trees. If you already have a mortgage, you can use the same strategy if you are still in the first ten years of a thirty year mortgage.

However, if you have twenty years or less remaining on your mortgage, it is time for a new financial strategy that reflects the economic realities of a society where jobs are transient and people, whether willingly or not, move more often than ever before.

Chapter Thirty-Eight

How to Beat the House

*We are not so much trying to make a place for
ourselves in the world as we are trying to make
a place for the world in ourselves.*

—Marianne Williamson

Paying more than the scheduled mortgage payment in order to reduce the term of a mortgage is not without risk because jobs have become every bit as mobile as people in our new society. And, as likely as we are to move from place to place, we are even more likely to change jobs.

It is often the case that we change jobs because we have no choice in the matter and often we move to find work after losing our job. Millions of jobs have been moved overseas for a variety of reasons but mainly to save costs; American labor is simply more expensive than labor rates in developing nations.

Corporate America is more driven than ever by the bottom line and we are our own worst enemies in this regard. Because so many of us are so invested in the stock market, we want companies to be as profitable as possible. This is what has driven jobs to foreign markets. We don't like that aspect of our investments but we can't have our cake and eat it, too!

The increased mobility of both jobs and people requires a strategy to maintain a higher degree of financial liquidity longer into our working lives than was the case only a decade ago. It is still sound financial planning that you plan to own your home mortgage-free before you retire but the new social realities dictate that you get there by another way.

I advocate nothing so much as the *thoughtful* deployment of your financial assets. If you think about the lessons of this book to this point, they are mostly about how to build your savings and thereby increase your level of financial security. And my fundamental premise is this: Never be too quick to let go of cash. There is not much that will enhance your financial peace of mind quite like money in the bank and that fundamental premise is the foundation upon which I have built the financial strategies that define *Money Well Saved*.

There is a saying in Mexico: plata mata carita. What that translates to, literally, makes little sense but, figuratively speaking, it means money trumps a handsome face. And what it implies is that appearances only count for so much in life. I know it is not real romantic but there it is.

And you have probably heard it said that cash is king. Now, *I* don't think "king" is the right word, exactly, but the sentiment, I do think, is correct—money does wield some power. And even a poet must live in the real world, after all, and that takes money—not flowery prose! All the strategies of this book lead to increased savings because money in the bank is the most certain path to financial security and peace of mind.

But money well spent is often money not spent at all and, so, in Step One, I detail thoughtful, considered spending. In Step Two, I shared a plan with you to save more from now on, even if you are unable to reduce your present expenses at all.

Then, in Step Three, I explained the need that we all have for a base amount of readily available cash to protect our financial viability in the event of unexpected job loss. It is the mobility of jobs in our new economy that have made our jobs more tenuous than ever and made the need for liquidity more important than ever, as I explained.

In Step Four, I explained why paying off your credit cards is not the most important consideration in financial planning and, again, why building your cash reserves should come first. Now, I want to detail how this same principle applies to mortgage debt, as well, and why I believe that it is more important than ever to increase your liquidity position by growing your savings—more important, even, than it is to pay down the principal balance on your mortgage if it has a remaining term of twenty years or less.

The foundation of this principle goes back to the financial concept of the endowment and the fact that saving the same amount of money but in different ways can produce entirely different outcomes.

The best way to gauge the impact of a financial decision is how it will affect your bottom line, that is, your net worth. But it is important that you consider all the relevant factors when doing so. For example, if your job is secure and you can count on your paycheck, it would seem to make sense that you could afford a lower amount of cash liquidity. But I would argue that cash is almost always better, regardless.

Again, think back to how institutions with endowments manage those endowments—their first priority is to grow the amount of that endowment because, the larger the endowment, the more income it will generate. Retirement is, basically, a period in your life when you live off the proceeds of your personal endowment. The money in your retirement nest egg, however, is different from a true endowment in one significant way—institutions will live forever.

Because people don't live forever, we can plan to spend down the principal as part of our retirement financial strategy (even if our heirs don't like it!). Institutions, on the other hand, do plan to go on forever and, so, avoid ever spending the principal portion of their endowment.

Your present day income, as a stream of income received paycheck by paycheck, can be thought of as the funding source of your personal endowment and you should consider the funding and growing of your endowment as one of your primary financial goals.

That being the case, you should never be too quick to spend money that can otherwise be used to grow your endowment; particularly while in the accumulation phase of your retirement plan.

For example, let's say you have a choice between funding your endowment and using that same amount of money to reduce the principal balance of your mortgage. Let's also assume that your mortgage has a remaining term of twenty years or less. How do you decide which is the better financial move? You judge the relative merits of each move by, first, looking at the effect of one versus the other on your bottom line—your net worth.

Let's say you have an *extra* $100 a month that you can either save or use to pay down the principal on your mortgage.

The immediate effect is largely the same in either case and your bottom line will be the same. When paid to principal, the long-term affect will be to increase the amount of each payment that goes to principal, from that point forward, for the life of the mortgage

If you take that same amount and add it to your endowment account, instead, it will begin to earn interest and compounded interest from that day forward. Compounded interest is interest earned on interest. In a tax-deferred account such as a 401(k) or an Individual Retirement Account (IRA, traditional or Roth), the power of compounded interest skews the equation in favor of saving and, so, is an even greater consideration.

Depending on the interest rate you are paying and the interest rate you are earning, you *are* likely to come out ahead, if only slightly, over time by investing in equity. But—here's the thing—money in the bank is a bird in the hand while equity sitting in a house is two birds in the bush because real estate *can* lose value.

It is entirely possible for the value of real estate to go down and take your equity down with it. Betting on equity is betting on the house but it is a real gamble, just the same. Do you remember my point about how the New Economy is characterized by nothing so much as job mobility? Well, nothing can kill a housing market in a city quicker than the loss of a major employer.

Meanwhile, money in the bank will always be there. And, yes, I know of the effect of inflation on cash reserves but, again, you don't need an infinite return on your cash in order to achieve a high level of financial viability, including, even, financial independence—just enough to cover your expenses! Any more than that is like frosting on a cake!

I advocate that your priority should be building your financial security and that is why I also advocate that building cash liquidity is a more sensible strategy than accelerated principal repayment *if* the remaining term of your mortgage is twenty year or less. Sure, paying interest costs money, but so does paying principal—you should never forget that. And remember, too, the financial principle known as opportunity cost.

When you weigh all the factors I have just described, you, too, will be forced to reconsider the wisdom of investing in equity and see the wisdom of a different strategy. Again, that strategy, in a nutshell, is, that as long as you have twenty years or less remaining on your mortgage, invest in liquidity not equity.

The next section of the book, and the last of the Seven Steps, is about achieving the ultimate in financial peace of mind—living your life on your own terms. Step Seven is to *Have an Escape Plan.*

STEP SEVEN

Have an Escape Plan

Chapter Thirty-Nine

Night Ride Home

*There is only one success—to be able to live
your life in your own way.*

—Christopher Morley

Back in the days when I was living through my own
financial meltdown, I started down the long road to recovery
with no real idea of where I was going. I was something like
Alice, lost in Wonderland, just trying to get someplace different
because I was so not comfortable where I was.

All I was really certain of at the time was that I wanted
to relieve some of the stress I was experiencing due to the way I
had managed my money up to that point in my life. When I
started down the path to financial peace of mind, it was with a
single thought in mind—that I would have been much better off
if only I had managed to save some of what I had earned.

Some revelation, right? But, that being my one light in
the darkness, the first step I took was in the direction of that

light. And that step, manifested in the real world, was that I simply began to pay myself first.

The path from that point forward, however, did not reveal itself. I had nothing more than the vague notion that money saved was a place to start but I sensed, as well, that there was more I had to learn. Since that time, I have come to understand that there is an art, a science, and a craft to money well saved.

But I have also come to realize that my instincts were correct—saving money *is* the first step towards greater financial peace of mind. And I did make a commitment to save a part of all I earned but, as far as having any financial goals at the time, that was it. I know *now* that a goal simply to save is not well enough defined to be of any real use and, in that respect, it was hardly a goal at all.

But the more I learned through my reading and research, and the more experience I gained as I worked through my own financial issues, the more apparent the way forward became.

In fact, my financial recovery turned out to be a lot like driving at night. When you drive at night, your headlights only clearly illuminate the next forty yards or so of road in front of you. Beyond that distance the road is less well illuminated and, beyond that, there is only darkness. But, in that way, we are able to get where we are going. (I have E.L. Doctorow to thank for that analogy.)

And that is how I made my way down the road I was on, as well. And, over time, as I honed my ability to manage my money, I also got better at being able to define my goals. Finally, one day, it came to me what my ultimate financial goal was and that moment was my personal financial epiphany and the last piece of my financial puzzle.

Before that realization, my goals were simply to save more and get out of debt. It was only later that I came to realize that those goals, as significant as they are, were only stops along the way. They were not my ultimate financial destination. The ultimate destination of the road I was traveling was financial independence.

Financial independence is simply having a source of income sufficient to meet your expenses that is *independent* of money earned through paid employment. You are financially independent when you no longer need to work for a living.

If you think about it, in order to retire, you will first need to achieve financial independence. Conversely, as long as you need to keep working to pay the bills, you will never be able to retire.

But retirement is usually perceived as something people of a certain age *do*, there is not, however, that same age association with financial independence. Work is an option at any age as long as you are financially independent and never an option if you are not.

Chapter Forty

What Color Are Your Handcuffs?

I don't have anything against work. I just figure,
why deprive somebody who really enjoys it?

—Dobie Gillis

There is another aspect of jobs in the new economic reality that we must all consider as we craft our personal financial strategy and that is that there is no real job security. Many in the first wave of the baby boom generation enjoyed lifetime employment with a single employer but, these days, few of us will experience that luxury.

In fact, experts in the employment field estimate that those entering the job market today can expect to have, on average, seven different employers during their working life. The downside of that statistic is that some of those changes of employment are likely to be involuntary.

Even if you are someone who can surf change, all that moving around can exact a toll. The fact is that most of us feel most at peace when we feel most secure; unwelcome change, in particular, comes as a jolt to many of us but there it is—the brave new world of work.

Surveys taken early in our new millennium reveal a growing level of job dissatisfaction and they also reveal that seventy percent of us would accept less income for more free time. Those sentiments are a reflection of nothing so much, I think, than of our human nature. Work is a good thing but there is such a thing as too much of a good thing and even a "good" job can be nothing more than a gilded cage, or worse, if there is something else you would rather be doing.

And even a job that pays well or provides good benefits can still be a lousy job. I mean, dangerous jobs, for example, are hardly worth the risk whatever they pay. But there is physical danger and, then, there are jobs that present a different sort of risk.

Most of us who have been in the work force for any length of time have wished, at one time or another, that we could simply walk away from the rat race but stayed simply because we could not afford to quit.

When you can't afford to quit a job because you need the money you are, in effect, bound by golden handcuffs. Some of us are lucky enough to make the transition from a bad job to a better job, but not everyone is lucky enough to make even that much of an escape. Those of us who stay in a job we would rather leave live the life of Sisyphus; the life of quiet desperation of which Thoreau wrote long ago.

But even in the best of situations, paid employment assigns the employee to a certain prescribed role that is contrary to the ultimate expression of human nature. That we are able to work in a cage does not detract from the fact that we are working in a cage! That being the case, we should strive to find our individual and most ideal balance between the need to earn a living and the demands of working for that living.

Let me here define the words *work* and *job* as the two do not mean the same thing, as I use them. Work is what we do to accomplish a necessary task. A job is a set of tasks defined by an employer and that we do in exchange for pay.

You can clean your house and it will involve work but it is not a job, as I define it, because no one is paying you to do it. A person can, however, have a job cleaning houses and it will be how they earn a living. All jobs involve work but not all the work we do is as part of paid employment.

Working for a living to the traditional age of retirement, or even longer, is a trap. Most of us fall into the trap simply because we fail to figure out that there are options that will provide the very same life and that are a much better bargain.

In essence, the working-class in Western society is hustling for a lifestyle that can be had for an on-going cost of somewhere in the neighborhood of $15,000 a year. If you are paying more than that, you're wasting your money and your time. And, because time is the stuff of life, when you waste money you are wasting your life.

I can hear your howls of protest, "$15,000 a year!" No way, right? The fact is that a middle-class life in the USA these days is basically food, shelter and transportation. And the difference between those who earn a lower middle-class income and those earning at the high end of that bracket is the difference between a used Ford and a new Lexus. But guess what? Everyone gets where they're going!

In other words, the difference between high income and low is not really all that much and, as long as you need to work for a living, you will live handcuffed to the contrived and artificial world of work that is often referred to as the rat race.

But there are viable and practical alternatives to the rat race and these alternatives have always been "out there." And these options are available to anyone. In fact, you have probably lived some version of one or more of the alternatives in your own life. If you were ever a college student, working part-time and subsisting on a diet of rice and beans, you have lived one of those options—it's called living cheap and that's an option.

Frugal living is another alternative that can allow you to work less and live more. Living cheap is one thing but living frugally is something else, altogether. Frugal living is the foundation of work on your own terms. And the foundation of frugal living is to consciously eliminate wasteful spending from your life, entirely.

I would guess that, on average, the unconscious middle-income spender wastes something like fifty percent of his or her earned income. That being the case, this means that the conscious spender can live on one-half of that same middle-class income.

Which means that, if wage income is what you depend on to pay the bills, you should be able to work half as much if, and this is a big if, you do it right. And by "right" what I mean is *thoughtfully*. Let me explain.

The average household income in the USA in 2002 was just about $48,000. On average, thirty percent comes right off the top to pay all the various taxes that are levied on earned income. Then, twenty-five percent of our income is spent on housing and, again, this is an average—your mileage may vary! What those two numbers reveal is that, before you ever even see your check, over one-half of it is already gone!

But we have not yet completed this exercise. Transportation, on average, eats up another fifteen percent of our income. That fifteen percent includes car payments, maintenance, and operation costs such as fuel and insurance. Are you keeping track? If you are, you now realize that the combined costs of housing, taxes, and transportation, on average, account for something like seventy percent of our income!

But the point I am making here is that the remaining thirty percent must pay for everything else! Thirty percent of the average income figure I cited earlier is $14,400. And that is all most of us have, on average, to pay for food, clothing, and everything else including the funding of the savings necessary to provide for that time in our life when we hope to retire from the workforce.

If that is the bad news, it is also a beacon of light shining in our financial darkness because what it means is that if you can relieve yourself of the cost of housing, transportation, and taxes, you should be able to live on just thirty percent of what you are earning today!

Well, guess what? It is entirely possible to pay off all your debts, including your mortgage, years, even decades, sooner that you might think *if* you make that the focus of your financial plan! And, when you are debt-free, you can live on so little income that you can greatly reduce or, even, eliminate your income tax burden entirely!

But there is only one source of income that can escape being taxed at all. And what kind of income is that? Drum roll, please—interest income earned on your savings and other investments!

Chapter Forty-One

A Walk in the Woods

Oh, Lord, won't you buy me a Mercedes-Benz...

—Janice Joplin

Sometimes, as it has been said, you can't see the forest for the trees. And, sometimes, we get so caught up in the everyday details of living that we lose sight of the big picture. The big picture I have been trying to paint here is of a lifestyle free of the financial anxieties that plague too many modern lives.

So, what does the big picture look like at the level life is lived? It would be a life where your personal finances are not the cause of anxiety and worry but, rather, just another aspect of living like keeping the car clean and the yard mowed.

For sure, we all hope that our efforts to manage our financial resources will allow us to avoid the catastrophes that money regularly causes too many of us. You know, stuff like bankruptcy, foreclosure, and divorce. But what we're really after is to be at peace with money and the role it plays in our life.

A life at peace with money has certain characteristics and the seven steps each articulate one of those features. The main characteristic of financial peace of mind, however, is that the cost of your lifestyle, as a percentage of your income, is going down not up.

Think about that for a moment—going down not up. If you think about how most people run their finances, as soon as their income goes up so do their expenses. Some up us even spend our anticipated raises before we actually get them!

But if you simply follow the tenets embodied in Steps One and Two, the percentage of your gross income that goes to support your lifestyle will actually go down while, at the same time, the actual amount of income available to do so will be going up. We covered this material before but it is so important that I want to go over it once more for you.

By following Step One, you will discover where your money is actually going and this enables you to decide what amount of that spending is money well spent and which is not. Then, using the tools I introduce such as the spending diary and spending plan, you look for expenses to reduce or eliminate in order to increase your savings.

Step Two is a plan to save more simply by planning to save one-half of every raise you receive from now on. When you are saving one-half of every raise you receive, then the equation will look like this:

For the sake of example we will assume that your present gross income is $50,000, that you are presently saving ten percent of that, $5,000. Now, let's say you receive a four percent raise. This means that your salary after that raise will be $52,000. $1,000 of the $2,000 gross amount of the raise will be added to the amount you are already saving ($5,000) and the other $1,000 can be added to spending (this includes any increase in taxes).

By following The Fifty Percent Plan, you will be able to finance both a higher standard of living and increased savings. Your savings would go from $5,000 before the raise to $6,000 after. $6,000 is equal to more than 11.5% of the amount of your new gross income and what that means is that your expenses, as a percentage of your income, have gone down from 90% to 88.5%. When this first came to me it was one of those *Aha!* moments—you can have your cake and eat it too!

Let's look at what happens the next year, assuming another raise in your income equal to four percent:

Your gross would climb to $54,080 and your savings to $7,040. That amount would equal over 13% of your higher gross income while your expenses would represent only 87% of your income—at most—because no one is forcing you to add the other half of the raise to spending.

The Fifty Percent Plan is about as close as you can get to alchemy in real life! When you are living the Seven Steps you will enjoy a margin of peace that will be continually growing and you will have achieved the financial peace of mind that goes with it.

Steps Three through Five are all about getting your financial house in order. Everyone needs an emergency fund and we should all strive to be debt-free and debt-proof and your growing margin of peace will provide the savings to accomplish all three. In Step Six I detailed a way to build equity in your home that keeps your total cost of acquisition to a minimum while balancing that purchase with the wisdom of growing your personal endowment.

Now, in the last of the seven steps towards greater financial peace of mind, you are ready for the final and ultimate step towards greater financial peace of mind—financial independence!

As I have written, you have achieved financial independence when you don't have to work for a living because you have some other source of income sufficient to meet your financial needs. Let us now consider what financial independence can mean to you and why it is the ultimate goal of financial planning.

A friend of mine, let's call him Dave, recently sold his five year old Honda Accord and leased an E-Class Mercedes sedan. He had just finished paying off the loan on his Honda and had the option of enjoying five or, even, ten years of a car-payment-free life.

Also gone, when he decided to go with the Mercedes, was the opportunity to save the money he instead chose to spend on lease payments. His insurance bill also doubled when he made the switch.

All told, he was paying over $600 a month for the drive to work, which was about the only time he used the car. That amount did not include the extra he was spending on gasoline (the Honda had gotten about twice the gas mileage of the Mercedes) or other increased maintenance costs.

"You only live once," he exclaimed, showing me his new toy. What I didn't say was that you also only get one chance to save money at any particular point in time and that, if you do choose to save instead of spend, the clock starts running on the total amount of compounded interest your money will eventually earn you.

The money you spend today, instead of *save* today, will subtract from your eventual bottom line. But the impact of spending is particularly onerous when it is spending that could just as easily have been avoided.

Happiness is not a zero sum game. The amount of happiness in your life does not subtract from mine; your neighbor's happiness does not subtract from your own. But finances, on the other hand, are a zero sum game. And, like most games, there is the way the game is played by those who win and the way it is played by those who don't and "ne'er the twain shall meet," you know what I mean?

Money, however, does not come with instructions and contrary to what seems to be popular opinion, he (or she!) who dies with the most toys does not win—he just dies leaving a bunch of toys that those left to clean out the garage will sell for a lousy ten cents on the dollar!

In the first year of the lease on his shiny new Mercedes, my good buddy, Dave, will part company with something like eight *thousand* dollars by the time all the damage is tallied up. If he had, instead, just kept on driving his perfectly (more than) adequate Honda, he could have banked that amount, putting it to work earning interest for him.

Let me see...Dave was 35 years young at the time he entered into the sixty-month lease. If he had chosen to save that money, instead, and retired at age 65, that $37,500 he spent over the life of the lease would have grown to somewhere in the neighborhood of—are you ready for this?—$340,000! Now, that is quite a neighborhood. And it is also quite a price to pay for driving a Mercedes to work instead of a Honda.

My point, simply, is that, as easy as it is to spend money needlessly, it is not without its costs and the negative effect of needless spending is compounded over time because of the opportunity you give up to put your money to work earning you interest.

If Dave had simply chosen to keep his Honda, he could have saved a whole bunch of money over the next few years. And, years later, all that extra money would present him with some real attractive options.

For example, he could even decide to retire at 62 instead of 65, what with an extra three-hundred (plus) grand in the bank. And that, my friends, is an extra three years of life lived on your own terms and not tied to a desk somewhere at an age when the commute starts to feel a lot longer than it once did.

"Well, sure," I can almost hear you saying, "but I'm not rushing out to score a Mercedes anytime soon." But spending is spending and needless spending is adding up whether it's in big Mercedes-lease-payment size chunks or little "another-pair-of-shoes-you'll-wear-once-and-donate-to-some-charity-next-spring" size chunks.

A $10 do-dad here, a $10 do-dad there—it is all adding up and subtracting from what could be your eventual bottom line and dreams of retiring when you're still young enough to hike, and bike, and dance the night away.

Take the time, sometime, to add up all the unnecessary spending you indulged in over the last thirty days. How much would your monthly total add up to in a year? In ten years? Until the time you're 65? And, by the way, almost every dollar of interest you paid on consumer debt should be added to your "needless spending" tally.

Chapter Forty-Two

Getting Zen About Retirement Planning

*Retirement is wasted on the old and youth is
wasted on the young.*

—Overheard by someone somewhere once

Money not saved represents an opportunity lost to begin accumulating compounded interest. Financial peace of mind, like retirement planning tranquility, is something we accumulate over time, just like money in the bank. In fact, our level of financial peace of mind is directly linked to our savings.

A lot of people are sweating the load right now because they are forty or fifty years of age and haven't saved a dime towards retirement or know that what they have saved is not going to be enough. The secret to the redemptive power of compounded interest is that the sooner you begin to save the less a secure retirement, and financial independence, will cost you in out-of-pocket cash.

And, if you implement and adhere to the financial strategies detailed in this book you will not only achieve financial peace of mind, you will reach an almost Zen-like state about your retirement, even on a modest income. Getting Zen about your retirement planning is the second bit of money magic you will accomplish when you live the Seven Steps. By the usual age of retirement, if not sooner, the Seven Steps will allow you escape the rat race without a money care in the world.

The secret lies in the fact that the money you save actually serves two functions in your retirement planning. One, it provides a source of post-retirement income and, two, savings represent income that does not need to be replaced at retirement. The first function is fairly obvious and a part of all basic retirement planning. The second role that savings play is not so obvious and the power of it is often overlooked.

Retirement is financed by replacing the income you receive from your job with some other source of income. This replacement income is usually derived from some combination of three sources—Social Security payments, a private pension, and income from savings and investments.

Let's focus only on that third element, income from savings and investments.

The seed capital to both save and invest can only come from our income (let's leave windfall money out of this equation because most of us won't ever get any). The thing to remember is that any amount you are saving at retirement, because you are, basically, getting by "without" it, will not need to be *replaced* at retirement from some other source.

For example, if you are saving ten percent of your income at retirement, and living on ninety percent, then, obviously, that ninety percent is adequate to support your lifestyle while meeting your expenses.

What this means, to make this point another way, is that you don't have to replace 100% of your income because you are not spending 100% of your income—only ninety percent.

So, that ninety percent is all you will need to replace in order to maintain your lifestyle. The implications of this are very important in retirement planning and what it means is that the more you are saving at retirement, the less you will need to replace.

When you follow The Fifty Percent Plan, the percentage of your income that you will need to replace will decrease with every pay raise you receive. If at retirement you are saving twenty-five percent of your income, you will only need to replace *at most* seventy-five percent of it.

Certainly, you can see that the more you are saving at retirement the more affordable your retirement will be. The more affordable your retirement is, and the lower your expenses are at retirement, the more likely it is that you will actually be able to retire.

All the sudden you have real incentive to cut needless spending in order to grow your margin of peace! Do you see the how Step Two, alone, will almost magically make retirement much more possible and relieve a large part of your stress in planning to meet your retirement-income needs?

Now, let's say that you also plan to eliminate your mortgage by the time you retire. Doing so will further reduce the amount of income you will need to replace at retirement and the sooner you do pay it off the sooner you will have that much more to save.

For the sake of this example, let's assume that by spending more thoughtfully and following The Fifty Percent Plan, you are saving twenty-five percent of your gross income at retirement. Let's also assume that your monthly mortgage payment, on the day before you retire, is equal to twenty percent of your monthly income and that, following the tenets of *Money Well Saved*, you have planned it so that your final mortgage payment is due the day before you retire.

All this assuming means that your retirement will only cost you, at most, fifty-five percent of pre-retirement income because you no longer have that mortgage payment to support and, of course, you will not need to replace that twenty-five percent you are saving.

Income and employment tax considerations are likely to further reduce the amount of income you will need to replace by at least another ten percent. And there are still additional savings to be realized. Remember, when you are retired, you will not have any costs related to working—no commuting, no power lunches, no special tools or wardrobe to keep current.

The total amount of these costs can vary widely, depending on what kind of work you do and the length of your commute, but they will reduce the amount of job income you will need to replace in order to get free.

And remember, this is all before taking into consideration the other two-legs that will prop up your retirement stool—Social Security and pension income. If you earn only the minimum Social Security payment, that amount, alone, could well prove to be more than enough.

If you won the lottery today, would you go to work tomorrow? Well, guess what? You just got lucky!

Chapter Forty-Three

The Cost of Freedom

*It is never too late to be who you might have
been.*

—George Eliot

But retirement is not where I am taking you here. This road leads to financial independence. In fact, if you take the word "retirement" and substitute the words "financial independence," everything in the last chapter would still apply.

Financial independence is simply a financial state where you are no longer dependent on employment income to meet your living expenses. How much money would you need in order to achieve financial independence? Well, that equation can be as complex or simple as you want to make it.

If you go to a financial planner, they get paid to make it as complex as possible. That is not, necessarily, a bad thing; it is what it is. At the other end of the planning spectrum is the rule of thumb that says you will need to have savings equal to twenty times your annual cost of living assuming an annual return of at least five percent.

For example, let's say your cost of living is $25,000 a year. In that case, you would need twenty times that amount earning five percent interest to generate the amount of interest income sufficient to meet your income requirements. The math is real simple:

$$(\$25,000 \times 20) \times (5\%) = (\$500,000 \times 5\%) = \$25,000$$

Unfortunately, even though that equation appears to be financially sound at first glance, it is not actually that simple in the real world. You see, there are two wild cards that make the actual planning more complex than that: the actual average return you earn every year and the effect of inflation on your savings.

You see, in the real world, interest rates go up and down over time. That being the reality, it is not only possible, it is almost a certainty that you will earn less than a five percent return on your savings over any one year period. If you do and you still withdraw five percent, the balance of your principal will go down.

The easiest way to work around this is to withdraw no more than the total interest earned the previous year and thereby leave your principal untouched. The problem with this strategy is that you might not have earned enough to cover your expenses for the coming year.

Inflation will have an effect on your savings, as well. Inflation drives up the costs of goods and services and acts to make the same amount of money worth less tomorrow than it is today.

And, the fact is, inflation does not need to be very much on an annual basis to add up to a significant amount over a number of years. So, even if the rate of inflation is *only* one percent a year, after ten years of that steady creep your money is now buying just ninety percent of what it used to buy.

For people on a fixed income, inflation and interest rates are genuine concerns. The concern for someone planning to escape the rat race is how to deal with those two issues and still maintain your financial independence.

Well, the easy answer, and the one you are most likely to get from most financial planners, is to work longer so that you go out with a bigger nest egg. The obvious problem with that answer is that it means you will need to spend that many more years running the rat race.

What if you don't want to do that? Well, I pondered that very question for years and, the truth is, I came up with the very same answer—only with a spin to it that is redemptive in its power to liberate your genuine self!

Chapter Forty-Four

The Three Day Workweek

Your work is to discover your work and then
with all your heart to give yourself to it.

—Buddha

So, how do you escape the rat race and keep working at the same time? The answer is, what I call, The Three-Day Workweek. See, even if you enjoy your work, the traditional five-day workweek can be a real grind. If you don't like your job, or even if it is only the case that there is something else you would rather be doing, working five days a week can be a real drag.

When you don't enjoy your job, the work day seems to last forever and weekends seem to fly by. There is so much to do during those two days off that there doesn't seem to be enough time to do it all.

I spent years trying to address these issues in my own life. For much of that time, I thought the answer to the stress work caused me was to find more enjoyable work. And, believe me, I tried. In the years I have been in the workplace I have had three distinct careers and earned five college degrees; all this in search of work that wouldn't seem so much like...well, so much like work!

Then, one day it dawned on me—it wasn't the work that was the problem, it was the five days a week that it took to earn a living. Work, I recognized, is an important part of a full life and the workplace fills certain social needs most of us have. But I did not need to work five days a week to fulfill those needs.

No, for much of my life, the only reason I worked five days a week was because I *thought* I needed all five days worth of income. Throughout my life, regardless of how much money I was making at the time, that was how much I spent. And whenever my income went up so, too, did my spending. It just seemed as if that financial dynamic was an inescapable part of life. It is not!

About this same time, I started to think that the only way to escape the rat race was to achieve total financial independence. I remember thinking that, if I could simply replace earned income with interest earned on savings, I would no longer have to work for a living. But when I sat down to figure out how much money I would need in savings to achieve financial independence the number was staggering.

At the time, I was earning about $40,000 a year. When I did the math, I determined that in order to replace that amount with interest income, assuming I was earning five percent interest on my savings, I would need to put away $800,000! If I could manage to sock away, say, ten percent of my income a year, I figured I could save that amount in, oh, 200 years or so.

As soon as I got over my initial depression, I soon came to realize that total financial independence might not be the answer I was looking for.

And, besides, it wasn't really the work I minded. What I didn't like were those five-day workweeks and how they were wearing me down. What, I wondered, would it do to that $800,000 figure if I were to keep working, only work less?

And, if five-day workweeks were not the answer, what was? I mean, how much *would* I work if it was up to me? It had never been the case that I didn't want to work at all, I just wanted to work less and have more free time to pursue other interests outside of work.

A five-day workweek is a mix of seventy percent work and thirty percent free time. Except that it is not, not really. A big part of the traditional two-day weekend gets used up recovering from the previous week or getting ready for the coming week.

And, for me, it was often the case that, with all I had to get done in those two days, I was exhausted by Sunday night. But as exhausted as I was, I always seemed to have trouble falling asleep and I knew this was caused by the anxiety I felt about returning to work the next day. It is no mystery to me why most heart attacks strike on Monday morning!

Also, I had worked a job that had a schedule of four ten-hour days. Based on my experience working that schedule, I knew four-day workweeks were not the answer, either; not only were ten-hour days too long, three-day weekends still did not seem long enough.

So, knowing that four-day workweeks were not what I was after, I next turned my attention to the prospects of a three-day workweek. And, like I tend to do, I started by running the numbers.

Chapter Forty-Five

Crunching the Numbers, Closing the Gap

To love what you do and feel that it matters—
how could anything be more fun?

—Katherine Graham

Each day of a five day workweek represents twenty percent of total income. So, if I continued working three days a week, I would only need to replace forty percent of earned income with interest income. Instead of the $40,000 I had first figured, a three day workweek would cut that number down to $16,000.

While I was crunching these numbers it came to me that all you needed to do to arrive at the total amount of savings needed to provide any target amount of yearly interest income was to multiply the yearly amount by twenty, as I explained earlier. In this case, then, the amount I needed came to $320,000 ($16,000 multiplied by twenty). Still a big number, I know, but it was less than one-half of the original amount.

It was during this time that it also occurred to me that my three day income plus my interest income would not need to replace 100% of my five-day income. For one thing, I was saving about ten percent of what I earned at the time and quickly realized that I would not need to replace that ten percent as part of my escape plan.

When I came to this realization, it was, yet another, *Eureka!* moment. Every percentage of your gross income you don't spend reduces the amount of income you need to replace in your three-day workweek world.

Then, while pouring over my check stubs, I saw that I was paying almost eight percent of my gross income in employment taxes. Now, as long as I was working, I would be paying that same gross percentage but the absolute amount would be less. This lesser amount, when taken as a percentage of my gross pay, would represent additional savings that would not need to be replaced.

I quickly realized that the same principle applied to my state and federal taxes, as well, and I estimated that reduced taxes would represent a total savings of yet another ten percent that I would not need to replace when I switched to a three-day workweek.

When I added all those savings to the ten percent I was already putting away, I only need to replace $8,000 of earned income with interest income. $8,000 times twenty is $160,000. The more closely I examined the figures, the lower the numbers dropped! At this point, I started to take it for granted that it was likely that the number could be reduced even further. Could I, for example, save more?

I did not know where to start to answer that question but I was determined to figure out a way do just that—save more!

Because any amount by which I was able to reduce my spending would, likewise, reduce the total amount of the nest egg I needed. What if, for example, I could reduce my spending by another ten percent?

Punching the revised figures into my calculator revealed that, if I could save that additional ten percent, the total I would need to bank would be *down* to $80,000. And, even though that $80,000 figure was not (and is not) an inconsiderable amount, there were yet more considerations, at the time, that made that amount seem much less daunting, still!

For one thing, I already had a few thousand in the bank. I wasn't starting from zero and it is likely that you won't be, either. And, for another thing, once I had a firm goal in mind, it was as though the forces of the universe (serendipity?) aligned in my favor and my nest egg began to grow by leaps and bounds. Whereas before, every windfall, large or small, seemed to disappear, now those amounts went straight into my four-day weekend fund.

Eventually, I was able to save the amount of money I needed in just a few years. As it turns out, the less you need the sooner you will be able to get there! And, once that money was in the bank and earning interest, I was free to retire to the three-day workweek. However, when I did reach my savings goal, I was only two years from being eligible for a reduced pension from my employer, so, I didn't go right away.

But something sort of interesting happened to my attitude once that money was in the bank. It seemed like just knowing that I could go if I really, *really*, wanted to, I didn't seem to mind the daily routine quite as much. It was like, as soon as I knew the option of a three-day workweek existed, just the thought, itself, was somehow liberating.

The three-day workweek will also go a long way towards addressing concerns raised by inflation and fluctuating interest rates for anyone living on an otherwise fixed income. Because, when you do continue to work, even if *only* three days a week, your savings will actually grow during times of low inflation and higher interest rates and, so, provide more income (than a lesser amount would) when interest rates are lower.

Sound financial planning should not be about saving blindly only to die rich—it should be about living a life as closely aligned with your dreams as possible. And, if you are able to use your savings so that they enable you achieve your natural balance of work and leisure, the work you do choose will be less likely to ever feel like a rat race. And, after all, money well spent is simply a tool to build the life you want and, then, to live it your way.

Afterword

Afterword

Before enlightenment: chop wood, carry water.
After enlightenment: chop wood, carry water.

—Buddhist saying

It will be the same for you once you begin to live in alignment with the Seven Steps:

Before Seven Steps: chop wood, carry water, balance checkbook. After Seven Steps: chop wood, carry water, balance checkbook.

There is a lot of thought that goes into money well saved and when you understand that you will have grasped the Zen of personal financial management. But there is a craft and an art to it, as well, and, in this book, you have been introduced to seven steps towards managing your money with craftsmanship and art and towards greater financial peace of mind.

The Seven Steps are the foundational goals of personal financial management upon which to build your sturdy financial house:

Spend With a Purpose
Plan to Grow
Hope for the Best...
Pay the Minimum
Reserve Your Peace
Unscramble Your Nest Egg
Have an Escape Plan

The Seven Steps are also the path that will lead you to achieving your own personal financial goals, as well. And that journey, too, begins with saving what you can today and, then, growing that amount for the rest of your working life.

I want to thank you for taking the time to read this book and I hope, if nothing else, it has made you stop and think. Money can be funny sometimes but, sometimes, not funny ha-ha. It doesn't need to come down to that, though, and it won't if you are able to practice thoughtful spending—it really is that simple.

And, now, I cannot think of better words with which to close than those of the inscrutable Mr. Spock of the good ship *Enterprise*:

"Live long and prosper."

www.ingramcontent.com/pod-product-compliance
Lightning Source LLC
Chambersburg PA
CBHW071712170526
45165CB00005B/1986

* 9 7 8 1 4 8 1 1 3 9 6 1 8 *